THE COMPLETE BOOK OF

HOME DECORATING

THE COMPLETE BOOK OF
HOME DECORATING

BARBARA MAYER

FRIEDMAN/FAIRFAX
PUBLISHERS

A FRIEDMAN/FAIRFAX BOOK

© 1994 by Michael Friedman Publishing Group, Inc.

ISBN 1-56799-063-0

Editors: Suzanne DeRouen and Nathaniel Marunas
Art Director: Jeff Batzli
Designer: Stephen Bitti
Photography Editor: Grace How

Photographs on pages 238 and 241 are courtesy Cooper-Hewitt National Museum of Design,
Smithsonian Institution/Art Resource, NY:

P. 241 Scott Hyde
"Dragonfly" Light
New York, 1900–1910
Tiffany Studios
Leaded glass, gilt bronze
Gift of Mrs. Margaret Carnegie
Miller, 1977-111-lab

P. 238 John White
Thonet (firm)
Vienna, Austria
Rocking Chair, 19th century
Beechwood, cane 97 x 54 x 107"
Gift of the American Institute of Interior Designers, 1969-103-2

Typeset by Bookworks Plus
Color separations by United South Sea Graphic Art Co.
Printed and bound in China by Leefung-Asco Printers Ltd.

For bulk purchases and special sales, please contact:
Friedman/Fairfax Publishers
15 West 26 Street
New York, NY 10010
212/685-6610 FAX 212/685-1307

DEDICATION
For my brother, Michael Carson

ACKNOWLEDGMENTS

Whereas many disciplines have their academicians, the field of interior design has decorators. Not only are they on the front lines of practice, they are also the researchers and theorizers who evolve new and better methods of arranging, organizing, and beautifying the home.

In the twenty years or so during which I have been writing about interior design, the starting point for most good stories has been what one or several decorators are doing that is new, more effective, or unusually beautiful. Certainly this book could not have been written without the considerable aid of numerous decorators. I would like to acknowledge all those talented individuals who have helped to make this book (and so many more) a reality.

CONTENTS

New Approaches for a New Decade

IMAGINE COMING HOME from a hard day's work. You turn the key in the lock, flick on the lights, and put parcels and mail down on the console table in the foyer before you hang up your coat. Nobody's home, but you check the bulletin board in the kitchen and see that the kids have after-school activities and will be home in an hour or so and your spouse has a meeting.

With everyone accounted for, you can enjoy the prospect of some relaxation time. So you change into casual clothes and settle down with a cup of tea and a book. The chair is comfortable, the light good, the surroundings peaceful.

This little image is one of so many scenarios, all different, in which somebody is seen enjoying his or her home. *Enjoy* is the key word here.

Decorating for the nineties has a similar function as in the past. Yet, there are differences. Beyond the spread of information and expansion of choices in furnishings and finishes, there is another, more profound change that goes to the heart of the matter. Decorating is something we do for ourselves more than others. Those Joneses we were once so busy keeping up with have moved away. Their departure, with baggage filled with rules about propriety, has given home decoration a freer cast. Another departure from the past is the concern for convenience, health, and safety.

More convenient homes

Electronic devices such as remote controls, timers, induction cooktops, and advanced materials such as low-emissivity windows are making our lives more convenient. Developments in the nineties will turn the already existing technology into systems that work together to produce what is being called the smart home.

More people will be turning lights and appliances on and off with a computer keyboard, telephone, or voice command. You will be controlling the sound you hear, changing the radio station or music source from any place in the house. Your windows and their coverings will open and close on cue, depending on the time of day and weather conditions. Outdoor lights will turn on at dusk and turn off when you go to

■ *OPPOSITE PAGE:*
This foyer strikes a balance between luxurious design and everyday practicality; it introduces a magnificent home, but provides a space for the mail.

bed. Electronic home security systems will foil intruders by not recognizing their voices. Mail will be delivered electronically. You will shop at home via a computer network.

Innovations such as these are bound to affect the way the home is arranged and decorated. Among the newer decorating questions are these: Which fabrics and colors minimize the glare from a computer screen? Which chair supports the torso best to protect against backache brought on by many hours spent in front of a computer? How do I arrange the kitchen to make room for more appliances?

Healthier homes

Making homes less hazardous to the health is surely an excellent idea with a serious purpose. It's only by changing our own homes that we can save the environment, states British architect David Pearson, author of *The Natural House Book*. In a similar

■ *BELOW, RIGHT:*
A brave new world of high-style electronics will combine home entertainment, security, and functional equipment into one system.

■ *BELOW:*
Someday, a panel like this one will put the controls to every appliance in the house at your fingertips.

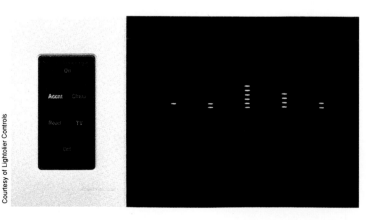

Courtesy of Lightolier Controls

vein, American architect Michael McDonough says that it's difficult for him to consider a place beautiful if it causes sickness or pollutes the environment.

In a rush to apply laboratory results to practical home decorating, however, some self-styled guides may be going too far. It's premature to suggest that a change of room color can lead to behavioral alterations. Perhaps some of these claims are more amusing than practical. We don't know how it was determined that flies don't like pale blue, that people work better in rooms painted light brown, that green is a good color if you've relocated recently, or that pink walls inhibit aggressive behavior.

The findings may be proven beyond a doubt. However, instead of painting a room pale blue to get rid of flies, why not add new screens? We can imagine a light brown room with poor traffic patterns and a cramped floor plan in which work is almost impossible. Providing a comfortable home seems more effective than painting a room green or pink to reduce tensions that might lead to aggressive behavior.

The point of view that considers, for example, how to minimize toxic fumes from building materials, paints, and finishes reveals a highly beneficial new way of thinking.

Some professionals are exploring how changes in building products and methods could reduce the burden on the environment. Besides installing passive and active solar collectors that save fossil fuels, other design decisions that can have an effect include placing windows so as to minimize the need for artificial lighting in the daytime and painting walls with nontoxic paints free of volatile organic compounds like formaldehyde. Hardwoods can come from well-managed plantations that are regularly replanted. Natural wood finishes such as linseed oil, citrus peel oil, juniper berries, and rosemary can be used. Full-spectrum light bulbs, untreated jute carpet underlayments, and houseplants used as natural air filters also are said to offer benefits that go beyond the front door.

Limiting your use of synthetics, especially if someone in the household has special sensitivity, seems perfectly sensible. Hardwood floors, wool or cotton rugs, solid

General Electric's "plastic" home (about one third is plastic) showcases plastic materials and new methods of building.

wood furniture put together without glue, upholstered furniture stuffed with cotton batting, untreated cotton window coverings, and latex paint in a light color to enhance available light are among choices considered by some authorities as healthier.

Choosing nontoxic and nonpolluting materials often is more costly. The builders of one home found it raised costs by about 25 percent. However, the movement to save the planet and our physical health is in its infancy and it seems reasonable to assume that the wish to achieve a more healthful home environment will produce desirable improvements.

One idea being advanced is that new items such as bedding, upholstery, carpeting, and wood furniture should air out for a while before they go into a home so any chemicals have a chance to dissipate.

An experimental plastic house built by General Electric could conserve wood, iron, and rubber if it were to be mass-produced, according to the company. GE says there is little waste since scraps used to build the house are recycled. A kitchen disposal unit converts a mountain of plastic packaging into recyclable pellets.

Even without special technology, decorating can make a difference in health in areas such as noise control. Unpleasant noises attend the use of appliances and the activities of daily living and leisure. Bells and buzzers go off and other people's music and television programs can crescendo into cacophony. Medical studies have recently indicated that excessive noise leads to increased physical and mental stress, interferes with concentration and sleep, and causes accidents.

Decorating materials can produce a more serene environment by muffling noise. You have to determine whether the problem is inside the room or outside it. If the noise is coming from within, you can minimize it with sound-absorbing soft surfaces such as carpet and fabric. If it is coming from outside, add insulation with book-filled shelves lined up against the outside wall and replace hollow-core doors with solid, sturdier doors.

In order to make a client's bedroom a quiet haven, New York decorator John Saladino used extra fabric and chose a subdued color scheme. First he installed sisal carpeting in a natural, pale brown shade. On it he placed a small wool oriental rug. The walls were padded with cotton batting and then covered with fabric. A quilt was hung above the bed mostly as decoration but also to deaden the sound. A cloth-covered table and upholstered easy chair completed the furnishings. The colors, faded periwinkle blue and wheat, contributed to the tranquility necessary for a comfortable bedroom. As this example shows, decorating with care and knowledge has ramifications that go beneath the surface.

A DECORATING PHILOSOPHY

If you think of your home in terms of how you can improve it, you will be at least a quarter of the way toward achieving a comfortable environment. As with everything from baking a pie to living within a budget, a step-by-step plan makes the seemingly impossible very feasible.

By the time you've finished reading this book, you will have learned the basics of planning any home, regardless of budget, personal decorating tastes, and time at your disposal for the task. Armed with this knowledge, you will be equipped to develop your own plan for a single room or an entire house.

There are many paths to success and a few well-trodden paths to failure. Before we start, let's eliminate some of the common roadblocks.

Never buy something you don't like with the idea you will throw it out in a few years when you get something better.

For their first apartment, Debbie and John bought furniture whose only virtue was its low cost. They thought they'd soon replace the pieces or that they would wear out. A decade later, the furniture was still with them—steadily more threadbare, but still serviceable. They finally gave it away.

Decorate for the person you are, not the person you want to be.

Don't use the furniture and decorating scheme as the time to reform what you regard as bad habits. Decorate for the person you are and the family you have. A happy home is a refuge, not a reform school.

Plan for the future.

We can't know the future, but we can suspect that we will be making changes. Make smart choices based on likely future plans. Many types of furniture—seating and storage furniture, for example—come in modular sections that are easier to move than larger units if you have relocation plans. Anything can be moved if it has to be, but life will be easier if you don't buy a grand piano right before accepting a new job in Hawaii.

These few sensible precepts are evidence of the new wave of freedom in home decoration. Years ago, there was a prescribed right way of decorating to which one had to conform. Today we take a more relaxed approach and recognize many different ways of life and styles. Furthermore, whereas once the authentic period room was the most desired type of room, country-style decorating is common today. That's good news for amateurs, since it doesn't call for an extensive knowledge of decorating history.

One factor supporting the growth of choices is the revolution in materials—paint formulas that can be matched by computer to existing paint and durable fabrics and carpeting that can be made fire-retardant and stain-resistant. Many fabrics now are labeled to indicate durability.

Decorating for yourself is easier than it used to be because of the proliferation of information—books, magazines, adult education and mail-order courses, and professional design schools are sources of guidance. Historic house museums are an excellent source of visual information, and their curators sometimes can answer questions or steer you to a good book for information.

If you prefer to decorate without consultation, you still have access to some of the top design talent in the country by purchasing professionally coordinated collections of fabrics, wall coverings, furniture, and accessories. You can browse through pattern books to find out about coordinated product lines.

Despite all the available help, however, you may still feel overwhelmed, inadequate to solve your decorating problems, and fearful that you are about to waste time and money and still not be satisfied. In that case, it is reassuring to realize that many professional decorators say they never outgrow the fear that when they get it all together, they won't like the results. They persevere, however, knowing that the more experience they amass in making selections, the easier it gets.

■
Coordinated collections from retail stores can take the place of a decorator. This collection of bedroom furniture and accessories is from the Spiegel mail order catalog.

I*Part One*
T ALL STARTS WITH YOU

■

Wallpaper books offer decorating ideas. This room setting was created around a wallpaper pattern from Sandpiper Studios.

Introduction

■

A successful room will always betray the amount of time that went into creating it; despite its simplicity, this design involved considerations of window treatment, color arrangement, furniture type and placement, and accessories, to name just a few elements.

■ What style home do you want?
■ Where will you go shopping?
■ What furnishings do you need to buy?
■ How much will it all cost?
■ How will you know you're getting good quality?

IN THIS SECTION we will answer all of these questions that are generally part of any home decorating project, be it one room or an entire residence.

We begin by showing how to take an inventory. A systematic review of what you have to work with, both in terms of space and in terms of furnishings you may already own, is generally the first step in any decorating project.

Knowing generally what size your rooms are, and about how much you can afford to spend to furnish them, and more or less what colors you like is fine when you're discussing redecorating at a dinner party. When making purchase decisions, however, it's necessary to be considerably more specific.

Among the topics to be mastered are: where to go for decorating ideas; how to measure your room; how to make a floor plan and a room scheme; how to decide whether to keep or jettison the things you happen to own; and how to analyze and divide up the various steps that lead to a satisfactory completed project.

Setting personal priorities is the most important step in achieving a decorating scheme that works. Only when you are clear on what you want and need are you ready to go out in the marketplace to find it.

In Chapter Two, we look in detail at the resources in the marketplace that are available to guide you. We consider the pros and cons of hiring a decorator. Choosing to do your own decorating doesn't close off other avenues of help, however, since various methods of guidance exist.

You also need to know how to set a budget and what financing might be available and about the variety of retail outlets that sell home furnishings and what specific advantages each type offers.

What is the advantage of buying at an auction? The answer is immediate delivery and, perhaps, a bargain.

Where can you find instant funiture when you don't have time to wait for delivery? One place may be your local furniture store where the floor samples may be on sale at a reduced price.

Knowing how to judge quality in furniture is an important part of being satisfied with what you eventually purchase. Often, however, one can't afford to pay for the very best quality. The shortcuts that cut down on cost without drastically curtailing function are all covered here.

■ *There are tricks of the trade that you will find yourself using all the time, once you've become familiar with them; this room, for instance, was doubled in size by the simple addition of a wall-size mirror.*

Chapter 1

Making a Decorating Plan

MOST PEOPLE KNOW more than they think they do about what goes into a good decorating plan. If the thought of making one for yourself is intimidating, realize that the process calls for many of the same skills as devising a household budget or estimating your net worth. After summarizing your needs and your assets, make decisions that best marry the two. You would expect to put a financial budget in writing. Adopt the same course for a decorating plan, since there will be far too many details to remember, even if you're doing only one room.

If you are starting from scratch and don't have much furniture yet, think first about what you need and what you would like. If you have some furnishings already, it's often more useful to start by taking stock of them.

Many people begin a decorating project knowing what style of furnishings they want. They may already have furniture and accessories reflecting that style. A surprisingly large number, however, do not have a clear picture of the style they want. Decorating is a visual and tactile medium, and you can improve your knowledge about it by looking at things, rather than just reading about them. The rooms you encounter in stores, in other people's homes, and in museums may be more meaningful than those you look at in pictures. However, you'll benefit by collecting ideas you like from books and magazines. So get a notebook in which to jot down ideas and paste pictures. The notebook can also serve as the place to keep room measurements, names of stores, lists of furnishings you own or need, and summaries of your other projects. When you're in the shopping phase, a portable file will be vital for spur-of-the-moment decisions.

Begin to build a library of ideas by browsing in decorating books and magazines. If possible, get some back issues of magazines that you can cut up for your scrapbook. Write down good ideas and keep track of colors you like. When you do choose wallpaper, paint colors, and a color scheme for an entire room, get a small sample of each of your choices to paste into the book. One way to organize it is with a section for each room.

Instead of planning to "redo the downstairs," break the job into specific projects such as choosing a living-room color scheme or organizing a storage wall. Figure out a project that is small enough to keep your blood pressure stable but large enough to make an impact; then do another. Completing the small projects can give you confidence for more complex tasks.

What decorating projects should you undertake? Here are some examples that run the gamut in terms of complexity and cost.

- Retile the bathroom
- Redo master bedroom
- Facelift for kitchen
- Furnish apartment from scratch
- Redo living room and add entertainment center
- Turn child's bedroom into a home office
- New lighting for living room or kitchen
- Create laundry room
- Turn basement into family room
- Make space for crafts

Finding a system that works for all these various projects is easier than you might think. All have certain requirements in common: evaluating what you have to work with; researching what is available and how much it costs; breaking down the job into furnishings needed and labor required; setting a realistic timetable in which to accomplish the task; settling on a budget; and, if necessary, obtaining financing.

You don't have to follow this particular order, but you do have to consider each of these specifics and eventually arrive at a definite plan of attack. Perhaps you can settle some of the issues right away. For example, you may know that the problem is the lighting in the living room, that as a renter you are precluded from installing permanent fixtures, and that the job has to be done on a tight budget.

This knowledge should lead you to ignore fixtures or track lighting, both of which are usually installed permanently, and to concentrate on moderately priced lamps. You might visit a few lighting stores to see what's available to buy and how much it costs. If

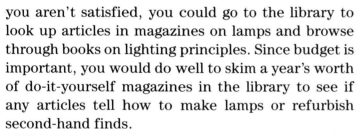

you aren't satisfied, you could go to the library to look up articles in magazines on lamps and browse through books on lighting principles. Since budget is important, you would do well to skim a year's worth of do-it-yourself magazines in the library to see if any articles tell how to make lamps or refurbish second-hand finds.

Whenever a job seems so large that it threatens to overwhelm you, back off for a while. Browse in books and magazines for decorating ideas; window-shop in retail stores to see what's generally available and how much it costs. Tell the store personnel that you are planning to furnish a new home and solicit their suggestions. Talk to others who have recently decorated their own place. Eventually, when you have some information, you'll be able to answer some of your questions about developing a plan.

WALK ON THE WILD SIDE

Grab a notebook and take a walk through the space that you will be decorating. You'll be doing this again and again, so don't worry about noticing everything. What you're looking for this first time is a list of assets (good view, large rooms, sunny, room for dining table in kitchen, and so on) and liabilities (too small, dark, no closet in bedroom, mismatched windows, for example).

What changes are essential for health and safety? Repairing a leaking pipe? Putting a safety lock on the door, or bars on the windows? What changes would be helpful? Moving the telephone and television connections? Adding or relocating electrical outlets? Removing a wall? Should you reclassify rooms—maybe turn the dining area into a home office, give the master bedroom to children to share, and turn a quiet back bedroom into a parental lair?

It will be helpful to have a floor plan of the space, in which windows, doors, heat registers, and electrical outlets are indicated. The room's dimensions (length, width, and height) should be carefully noted on the plan.

Professional designers work with three types of diagrams: an informal schematic drawing, a precise floor plan drawn to scale, and an elevation drawing that shows a side view of a structure, revealing how the space is organized vertically from bottom to top. An elevation drawing can be fairly complex, but a floor plan in which there is no vertical dimension is relatively easy for a beginner to execute, especially if you start with lined graph paper.

A schematic diagram in which you use a pencil to outline space that represents different activity areas can be a way of stimulating your creativity. Some rooms and activities are fixed. The kitchen location determines where food will be prepared. The bathroom is rarely movable without great expense. But the uses of other rooms can be changed. A schematic drawing might be useful in showing how to group all the noisy activities together in one area of the house. It could help you visualize why a home office should be moved to another location than the one you were planning or why the baby's room should be at the end of the hall and not right near the living room.

Once you've settled on appropriate space divisions, you'll need a floor plan. This accurate diagram of the dimensions of the space also records features such as windows and radiators and electrical outlets. Floor plans should be drawn to scale. A standard measure is a half-inch (1.3 cm) equals one foot (30 cm). You can also have each square on a piece of graph paper equal one foot or make the plan larger by allowing one inch (2.5 cm) to equal one foot (30 cm). On a half-inch (1.3-cm) scale, a room that actually is 12 by 16 feet (4 by 4.8 m) would be 6 by 8 inches (15 by 20 cm). If you used a quarter-inch (half-cm) scale, the same room would be 3 by 4 inches (7 by 10 cm) on paper.

Drawing to scale allows you to see each element in proper relation to all the others. You can use the floor plan to try out different arrangements of furniture (also drawn to scale), to see which are feasible and what size pieces work best. By noting such features as electrical outlets, you can see at a glance whether your planned arrangement is practical.

A floor plan is only as good as the accuracy of the actual measurements you take before constructing it. Plan to make at least two drawings. The first doesn't have to be carefully measured. Make an outline of the shape of the room as it looks. Then, working carefully with a folding yardstick, begin to take measurements. Do one complete wall at a time and allow for several sessions so you don't get tired. Ideally, ask your housemate or a friend to help you

■

It is always useful to have a floor plan of the room that you are designing; you will be surprised at how much can be accomplished on paper.

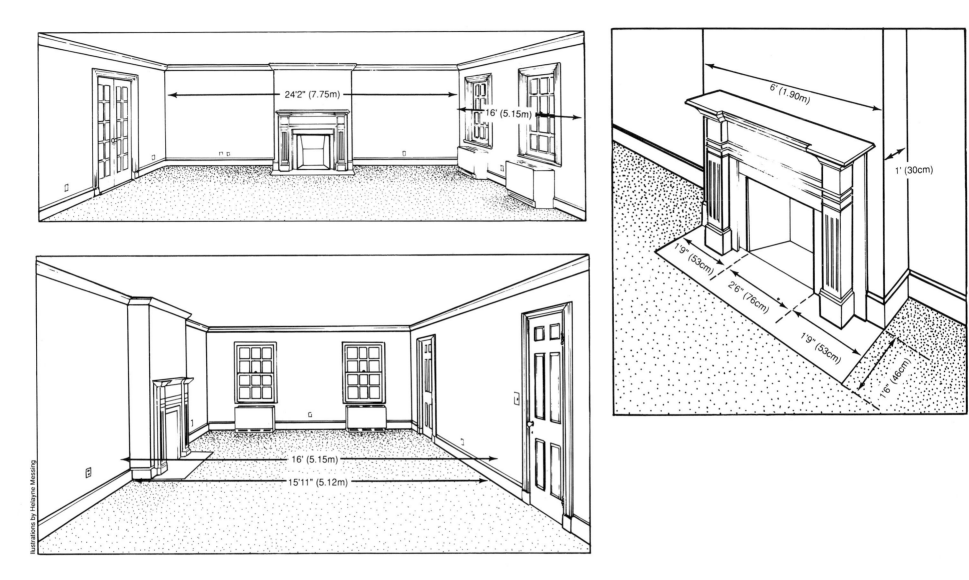

Illustrations by Helayne Messing

check each measurement for accuracy. You'll be measuring such things as walls, indentations and changes in floor level, doors and the way they open, windows, closets, cupboards, staircases, fireplaces, and bath fixtures. Electrical outlets and switches should be marked. If height is important—for example, how high a radiator is or where a window sill is located—measure it.

Once you have all the measurements you need, use a ruler to accurately draw the final plan to scale. Do the plan in dark ink and photocopy the drawing so you have several copies.

If you buy some tracing paper, you can place it over the plan and try out different room arrangements without messing up the diagram. A large roll of tracing paper frees you to experiment to your heart's content. A plan does not have to be elaborate, but it does have to be fairly accurate to be of any use.

Some people can get more out of a floor plan than others. If you can visualize the actual room from the scale drawing, shop in art-supply stores, bookstores, or home centers for aids to help you make a professional-looking floor plan. You can buy templates and cutouts that show typical furnishings—everything from a grand piano to an ottoman. Some of the templates are magnetic and stick on a board; others are paper cutouts. You will also find different kinds of rulers and drawing aids at some art-supply stores.

▪

The advantages of having detailed diagrams of the room you wish to design cannot be emphasized strongly enough; important decisions can be made before you even touch one piece of furniture.

SETTING PRIORITIES

What do you want in a home? A quiet refuge in which to retreat from the social and work world? A center for raising kids? A place to work as well as live? A showplace in which to entertain? A place to put your recycling and ecological concerns into practice? A center for maintaining your physical and mental health?

No two families are exactly alike, although we all have much in common. The decorating lesson learned by the end of the twentieth century is that no one scheme works for everyone. The most satisfying home is one that supports the people who live in it. To be sure you allow for your unique requirements, spend time considering them.

Consider these issues:
- Special needs of everyone in the household
- Preferred leisure activities
- How you'll entertain
- Where you like to eat
- Housekeeping style (sloppy, neat, compulsive)
- Feelings about the meaning of a home
- What's usable now or what needs repair
- How much money you wish to spend
- The time and skills you can bring to the job

Careful and considered answers to questions such as these can be surprisingly helpful in making decorating decisions almost self-evident. For example: If yours is a child-centered household, yet you prefer a neat and orderly house and enjoy entertaining elegantly, you will need to accommodate two fairly divergent sets of needs. One way to do it is with plenty of closed storage, a children's play area that can be closed off, and furniture that is durable without necessarily looking too rugged.

If, on the other hand, your style is more relaxed and your need for order is not so pressing, one large family area with casual furnishings is fine. If your favorite way to entertain is dinner parties for eight, you will need a large dining table and eight chairs. Those who would rarely give dinner parties can use the money they would otherwise spend on dining-room furniture for something else.

Information gathered in an inventory should be written down. It will help you crystallize your thoughts. Don't be surprised if you find yourself changing your mind about a number of long-held theories. Give yourself enough time in the inventory stage to make sure your selections are the ones you really want to make.

■
This imaginative children's room features a painted mural and a fanciful custom headboard.

What kind of space?

A residence may be open or closed in feeling. When there are only a few walls to mark off separate rooms, it's an open floor plan. When the space has been divided into separate rooms, each behind ceiling-high walls, it's a closed plan.

We've come full circle on attitudes about the arrangement of space. In all centuries prior to the current one, as affluence grew, the number of rooms in the house grew, too. A cave was an undifferentiated space and a true open-plan environment, but as civilization progressed, separate rooms were dedicated to sleeping, eating, and dining. The typical early New England Colonial farmhouse consisted of a main room downstairs as kitchen, dining, and living room, a second room for sleeping, and an upstairs loft where all the children slept. However,

■

An open-plan farmhouse is an informal space.

■ *RIGHT:*
An open plan along modern lines not only highlights space, but showcases efficiency as well.

■ *OPPOSITE PAGE:*
A window can give the illusion of greater space; white paint can be used for the same effect.

as the family became more prosperous, new rooms and wings were added. A mid-nineteenth-century town house had a bedroom for each family member, a morning room as well as a drawing room, and separate rooms for specialized activities such as sewing and flower arranging.

The modern sensibility tends to favor open-plan residences with only a few fixed partitions. Space, especially on the main floor where living room, dining area, and kitchen are centered, is organized to flow from one section to another, and access to the outdoors is part of the plan, if possible. Open plans offer a greater sense of spaciousness, especially in a small house where individual rooms would necessarily be small. They also are more flexible and can hold a few or many people equally well. They facilitate togetherness and end the isolation felt by, say, the one who is cooking dinner for the family. Their drawbacks include lack of privacy, noisiness, and a sense of being too big, even barnlike, and therefore cold. Wide-open spaces are also subject to draftiness.

Closed plans allow for much greater privacy and separation of activities, which may be essential when the residents' ages are disparate or when unrelated adults share a house. They make it possible to close off rooms that are not in use, which can make for good energy savings, but they lack flexibility and often engender a feeling of constriction.

Frequently you have no control over whether you live in a closed- or open-plan environment. But if the space you have is not the one you want, many options exist to help you minimize the drawbacks.

Overcoming some of the problems associated with an open plan is relatively easy through the use of partial walls, noise-absorbing surface materials, and the arrangement of furniture in zones or sections. If most of the house is on the open plan, make sure there is at least one spot that is a quiet refuge.

Minimize the claustrophobic feeling in closed-plan houses by taking down some walls, choosing light colors for surfaces, using a minimum of furniture and accessories, and adding a window or a skylight. Even the addition of more lighting can be helpful.

Moving around your space

Preparing a meal is just one of the frequent daily activities of living that requires movement through your space. You have to navigate between the sink, stove, refrigerator, and countertop to assemble the dishes. The food has to be brought to the table. The table has to be set and then cleared. Perhaps the kids habitually do their homework just before dinner. If they use the dining table for the task, there are bound to be conflicts as table setting interferes with a science project or vice versa.

Coming in from outdoors, taking off outerwear, getting the mail and putting it down, moving from one room to another, and many other activities force everyone in the household to follow a pathway. This movement is known as *circulation* in decorating. By planning for it, you can eliminate daily bottlenecks and make your home more comfortable and workable.

You can use a floor plan drawn to scale to check for bottlenecks in circulation before you actually place your furniture; it's easier to move a paper cutout of a sofa than the sofa itself. Once you've settled on a room arrangement, lay a piece of tracing paper over the floor plan and draw the lines of circulation.

The general principles are that pathways should be short and direct and go around and not through areas of work or play. You want people to be able to come to the dining table without walking between the sofa and easy chair. It would be nice to open the curtains each morning without tripping over a lamp cord. For safety, pathways on which you will be traveling encumbered with objects, such as the route from stove to table, should be free of obstacles.

Eliminating barriers

Barriers in the home should be eliminated not only for the sake of decorative appeal but also to ensure safety. As one commentator put it: "We are all temporarily able-bodied." Young children and frail elderly people are the most obvious beneficiaries of

■*BELOW:*
A typical circulation plan.

■*RIGHT:*
The kitchen can be one of the more dangerous rooms in the home; lessen the risk with lots of strong light.

a safer home environment, but everyone benefits from such changes. It's now known that the aging process starts early—noticeable physical changes begin to occur around age forty. So the emerging body of knowledge about how to compensate for aging with simple, often inexpensive alterations in home decor and furnishings is valuable for everyone.

The most common problem as one ages is loss of visual acuity, which is experienced by 95 percent of older adults. Hearing and manual dexterity also diminish with age. In general, it's possible to compensate for loss of visual acuity by installing more lighting, using lighter materials and colors in decorating, adding windows or skylights, and changing window treatments to permit more light to enter the house. It's especially helpful to install more lighting where people will be reading and writing, cooking or taking medication, and particularly on stairways and in the bathroom, which are the sites of numerous home accidents.

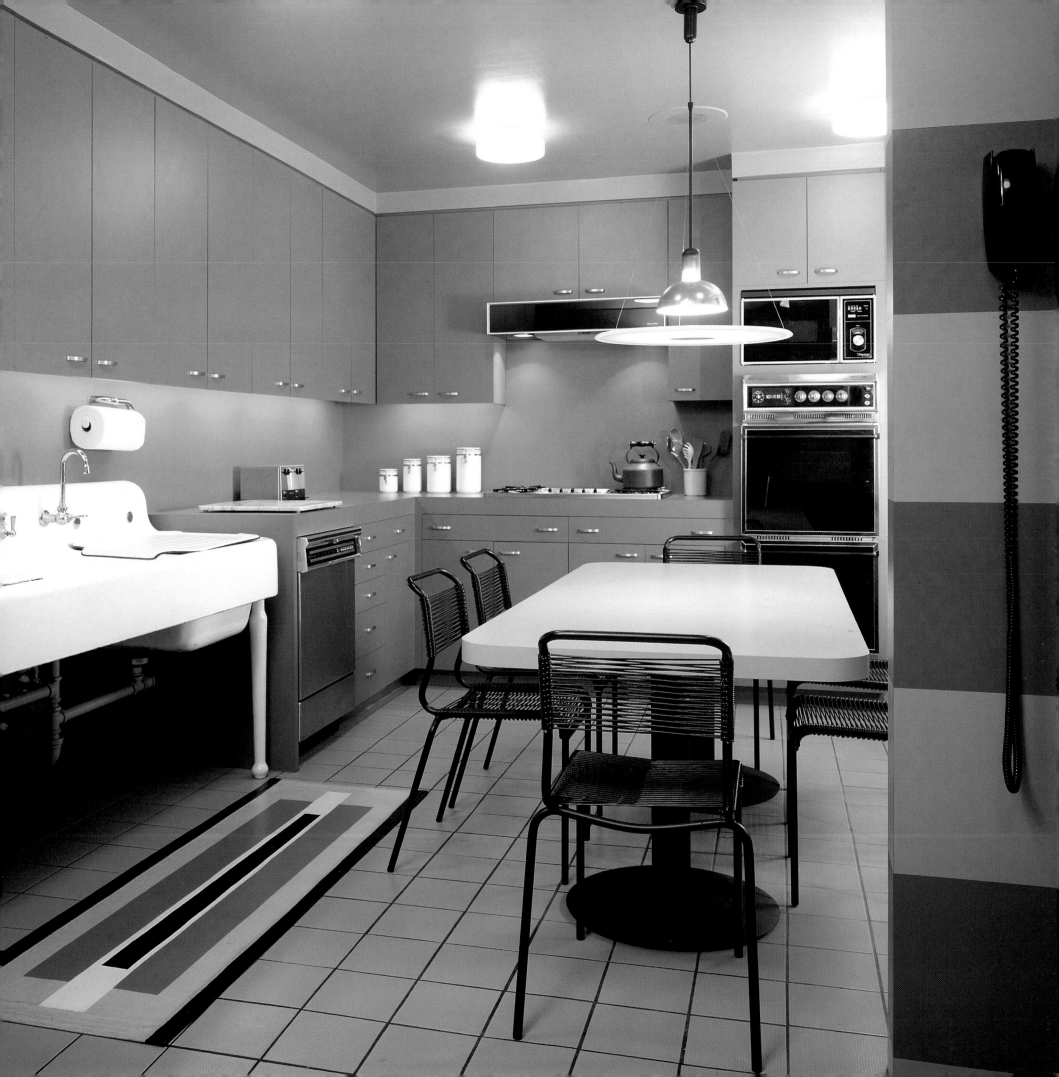

Besides adding more light, you can replace hard-to-decipher appliances, such as clocks with small numerals, with new models that are easier to read. Larger print compensates for a diminishing ability to focus on near objects. Even so simple a decorating idea as buying a decorative magnifying glass as an accessory can nullify the negative effects of being unable to make out the printing in the telephone directory and dictionary.

To control glare from the lights, which bothers people more as they grow older (then again, some people are just plain sensitive), cover windows with light-filtering blinds or shades. Blinds don't obstruct the view or entry of light. If new windows are being installed, investigate tinted glass, which can cut down on glare. Use translucent shades on all lamps and choose matte finishes for wall coverings and countertops instead of shiny materials.

It's easier to distinguish barriers such as furniture and steps if you contrast a light red or orange color against a darker blue or green. A room might have peach walls, white molding, and medium-blue carpeting, for example. (Safety hazards in particular rooms, such as the bath and kitchen, will be covered in Part Three, when we look at decorating room by room.) In general, however, smoke detectors and nontoxic and fire-retardant materials and fabrics can raise the level of safety in any household and protect its members.

Diminished hearing or the noise of the radio or television can make door bells, telephones, and alarms inaudible. Compensate with carpeting, upholstery, and fabric window treatments to absorb noise. If someone in the household is hard of hearing, place chairs closer together to make conversation easier.

To cut down on potential falls, remove scatter rugs or glue them down and rearrange furniture to eliminate booby traps such as low coffee tables and obstructions in front of windows. Rearrange cabinets so frequently used items are on low shelves that are easy to reach. Replace knobs on doors and cabinets with levers and C-shaped handles, which are much easier to grasp.

The types of furnishings that you buy can make a big difference in physical comfort. Choose seating that is easy to get into and out of, avoiding low, very deep upholstery. You can buy lamps that turn on and off at the touch of the base. You can purchase an adapter to convert any lamp with a metal base to go on and off by touch.

If you are remodeling a space or building, consider ways of eliminating barriers in each room. For example, you can remove sills and thresholds in interior doorways to reduce the chance of tripping. By relocating important features to a ground floor instead of the basement, you minimize the likelihood of tripping on the stairs. For example, move laundry equipment and the circuit breaker from their usual basement location to the first or second floor. Installing safety aids also repays the slight additional cost. Place handrails strong enough to bear a person's full weight on both sides of the stairs.

If a person in the household suffers a substantial disability and there's no money for needed major renovations, check with a governmental department on aging to see if low-interest or deferred-payment loans are available. Home-equity loans also can be a source of capital for home improvements.

■ *OPPOSITE PAGE:*
A window seat, particularly one of these dimensions, is a luxury that few houses can boast; it fully deserves an appropriately decorative treatment, with heavy drapes and plush cushions.

■ *BELOW:*
Elegant doorknobs and handles are among the most overlooked, yet most effective, decorative treatments for any room in the home.

Courtesy of Baldwin Hardware Corporation

Chapter 2

THE HOME DECORATING MARKETPLACE

■

Decorators can help you integrate a variety of accessories into a masterful whole.

SHOULD YOU HIRE A DECORATOR?

Not long ago, furnishing a home with the help of an independent professional decorator was the prerogative of older upper-income clients. Nowadays decorators work with a much greater client base, including busy professional couples who are used to consulting experts and have the funds to pay them.

Should you join the crowd and employ a decorator? How much will it cost and what are the advantages? Unfortunately, there are no simple answers to these questions. Decorators today often work in a variety of ways, depending on the situation. Some earn part or all of their fee in commissions on purchased merchandise, while others pass on some of their trade discounts to clients and charge an hourly rate for consultations. Many combine billing methods or tailor fees to specific jobs.

Some decorators specialize in a particular look; others believe their job is to translate the client's wishes into a finished interior. It's up to you, the client, to question a decorator before you engage him or her so that you are clear about how much you are paying and what you are getting for your money. A written contract can be helpful in enumerating rights and obligations on both sides. A clause that spells out how the agreement will be terminated in the event of disagreement is an important safeguard for both parties.

If you hire a decorator, you should receive guidance on selecting a color scheme and furnishings and placement of your furniture and accessories. Many decorators are qualified in space planning and can advise on lighting and acoustics. They may also have some ideas about adding on a room or a wing, although decorators do not substitute for architects.

Among the greatest advantages of employing a decorator is to gain help in coordinating the complexities when it comes to installing a variety of furnishings and completing carpentry and other construction. They can visualize how plans will look when the job is done, and often they can help you find craftsmen and sources for unusual furnishings.

Decorators say they actually save a client money and time by helping them make the right decisions.

Such claims have merit. Expertise as a rule does result in a more efficient use of time and money. To find the right advisor, you have a variety of options, which range from making calls to decorators listed in the telephone directory to seeking personal recommendations. It's important to see examples of a decorator's work and to feel a personal rapport with the individual. Since large sums of money may be involved, it's also essential to check the decorator's reputation.

■

By using a matching fabric and wallpaper you can achieve a decorator look without hiring a decorator.

Independent referral services for decorators have sprung up in many large cities. Usually these services charge no fee to the consumer. The decorators on their roster, who are also their clients, may pay a fee. A referral agency is a starting point since it gives you access to information about the fees and special skills of a number of individual decorators. However, you still should talk to other clients and check reputations before proceeding. To find the name of a referral service, check in the telephone directory. A number advertise in local magazines geared to affluent homeowners.

No matter how you find a decorator, it is important to feel comfortable with whomever you hire, since you will be working closely together. Many decorators are willing to talk to you without charge at a first meeting. Others may suggest they come to the home and provide some ideas for a small initial fee. If you are uncertain about whether you need or want a decorator, this type of consultation is a good way to test your interest in working with one.

Prepare for the meeting by writing down what you expect, what you need, and what you wish to spend. You will almost certainly be asked which problems you want to solve, which decorative styles you like, and how much money and time you expect to invest. If funds are scarce, ask about doing the job a little at a time.

A number of furniture and department stores offer decorating services. Advantages to using them include access to the resources of a large store, ability to charge all purchases, guarantees that the merchandise will arrive in good condition, and possible time savings in job completion. Some stores don't charge extra for decorating advice, provided a sufficient amount of merchandise is purchased. Since the retailer has had to hire the decorator, it's realistic to assume that you're paying for the service, perhaps in the store's pricing policies.

A mark of a very professional retail decorating department would be some or all of the following services: The designer will shop wholesale decorating sources for items not carried in stock; draw floor plans and make working drawings; design custom furniture; work with contractors and architects; help clients select linens, dinnerware, and accessories from other store departments.

There are substantial variations in the range of services offered in retail stores (and also by individual decorators) and the skills and training of the people who will help you. Since policies are varied, it's important to comparison-shop to find out what services are offered and how much they cost.

COORDINATED GALLERIES

You can still get help, even if you don't work with a decorator. A particular look in which pieces coordinate but don't necessarily match is available at brand-name furniture galleries. The idea behind the coordinated gallery collection put together by one manufacturer is that a retailer can concentrate on customer service, freed from many of the selection chores. The manufacturer also provides sales training and guidance in choosing accessories.

In some ways, a gallery duplicates the designer section found in women's ready-to-wear departments across the country. If you like the look, shopping is simplified because all the merchandise has been designed to go together. Some of the better-known gallery names in the United States are Ethan Allen, Drexel Heritage, Pennsylvania House, and Thomasville Furniture. Some of these American names can be found in other parts of the world.

Coordinated home furnishings collections bearing well-known designer names such as Laura Ashley, Ralph Lauren, and Jay Spectre also provide a specific look at products guaranteed to go together.

▪ *OPPOSITE PAGE:*
If the area around your home is interesting, bring it inside; with the doors open, this room extends all the way to the treeline.

A DECORATING BUDGET

A realistic decorating plan can't be made until you've considered how much to allocate to the project. If you will be financing it with a personal loan, which you'll repay over time, you'll need to consider how high a monthly bill you can afford. Besides personal loans from a bank or credit union, many retailers also advance credit. Naturally, you should compare interest charges and payment schedules before making a choice between these two methods of paying for home furnishings.

Ideally, you should allow plenty of time for furnishing and decorating. Choosing colors and materials and waiting for items such as custom-made window treatments is time-consuming. Most people decorate rarely, so they need to reflect a long time before they feel confident about making decisions.

A knowledgeable professional decorator can be helpful in explaining what furnishings cost and what features denote quality and durability. You can do your own comparison-shopping by looking in several different types of stores. Even if you are on a strict budget, it's a good idea to visit some of the better stores in town. A sale or an opportunity to purchase a piece over time may bring the better piece down to a price you can afford.

Novices worry that an expensive piece might show up the rest of the decor or that a costly piece of upholstery will get shabby long before the room can be completed. Usually, however, good furniture upgrades the rest of the room. As a rule, when furnishing over a long period, choose fewer, better pieces and be particularly careful to select durable fabrics and classic, unfaddish pieces.

A higher price is not always an indication of better quality. Price reflects all costs associated with manufacture including labor and raw materials. Raw silk is more expensive than close-weave cotton or nylon, but the latter two are much better choices in upholstery fabrics for a family with young children.

Decorating involves many skills, including mixing colors and arranging forms, so good design can be achieved on almost any budget. One approach to

Design: Bradshaw De Palma. ©image/dennis krukowski

saving money is to improvise furnishings at first, gradually replacing the makeshift pieces with others as you can afford them. Another idea is to buy only the essentials and add to them slowly.

An example of the first approach has you scouting secondhand furniture stores, thrift shops, and church sales. You might pick up an old sofa for a tiny sum or even find one that's free for the taking. Meanwhile, save enough money to buy a new sofa and discard the old one when you can. The second approach would be to buy large rectangular cushions and cover them in a durable fabric, such as sailcloth. At first you'd use them at floor level. While not comfortable for older folks, this ploy will do for those with young bones. The next step would be to build or buy a platform for the cushions. Finally, you could have the same cushions recovered in a more costly and attractive fabric.

A buying plan can be executed as quickly or as slowly as finances dictate. Once you've acquired a bed, dining table and chairs, lounge seating, and a few lamps, you have the basics.

■ *OPPOSITE PAGE:*
The charm of this room is achieved with the generous use of finery; notice how the draped curtains showcase the spacious bay window and its stunning view.

■ *ABOVE:*
A comfortable and inviting room doesn't have to be expensive to create; this room's warm look comes from the simplicity of its design.

■

A period look can be achieved with a minimum of expense if you are willing to take the time and effort to bid at an auction; in fact, sometimes it is the only way to find the items you want.

There are occasions when you need furniture fast. One solution is to buy showroom samples. What you see is what you get, and you can take it away with you in a truck or station wagon or arrange for quick delivery. Some retail stores also sell furniture in kits, which you take away in a box and put together yourself. If you haven't checked furniture stores recently, you'll be surprised to see what a wide variety of unassembled furniture is available. Most kit furniture is contemporary and has clean lines. But mixed with a few antiques, it can be part of a warm and inviting room. Used furniture and antique pieces are other options, especially if they are in good condition and can be set out immediately without refinishing or repair.

Auctions provide instant gratification since you can—and usually are required to—remove an item as soon as you've acquired it with the highest bid. It is often said that used and antique furniture, accessories, rugs, and artworks are available for a song at auction. This way of acquiring home furnishings requires you to do more homework than other methods, but it can be rewarding if you look over the items carefully ahead of time. Call ahead to find out the times of display in advance of the sale.

If there's a catalog, study it ahead of time and, when the item's cost warrants it, consider hiring an expert such as a local antiques dealer to examine the piece in question before bidding on it. Bargains usually come only to those who are knowledgeable, and the potential for disappointment is greater since there are normally no returns of items bought at auction.

If you want to bid and can't be present at the auction, you can leave an order bid. The current pattern is for the auction house to receive its payment from both consignor and buyer. The buyer usually pays a 10 percent surcharge on the final bid.

MAIL-ORDER BUYING

Home furnishings are among the many products available via mail order in some countries. You may see ads for catalogs in decorating magazines. Aside from the time saved, another reason for shopping via mail is the opportunity it presents to buy unusual merchandise that may not be available in your town. For example, only a few companies sell authentic reproduction items for home decor, such as fabrics, lighting fixtures and light bulbs, architectural moldings, and bath accessories. It is likely that these companies are not in your town, so you may need to order by mail.

One of the main reasons for buying furniture by mail is the opportunity to pay lower-than-standard retail prices. Some mail-order companies offer goods at prices that are at least 30 percent less than retail; these companies have lower costs and pass the savings on to their customers.

©image/dennis krukowski. Design: Charles Krewson

The rustic elegance of this room has been created through the careful selection of furniture and decorative items that suit its exposed wood beams and paneling.

■ *OPPOSITE PAGE, ABOVE:*
The stain on this rolltop desk perfectly complements the quiet elegance of this study.

■ *BELOW AND OPPOSITE PAGE, BELOW:*
The large selection of fabrics available today makes it possible to match the look of a room with your ideal vision of how it should be. Don't forget that texture is every bit as important as color.

However, there is a trade-off. What you give up includes decorating service and a chance to see and touch the furniture before buying it. Here are some questions that have to be answered before you place a mail order for furniture:

■ What happens if the furniture arrives damaged?
■ Is delivery included in the price? (It is usually not included and adds from 4 to 10 percent to the cost.)
■ What type of carrier is used? Does the carrier deliver the furniture to the home, unpack it, place it where it will be used, and remove the voluminous packaging?
■ How long a wait is there? If the date is not met, can the order be cancelled with full refund?
■ How can a sample be seen, especially if there is a choice of fabric or finish?
■ How much of a deposit is required and when does the balance have to be paid?
■ If service should be needed later on, is any available?

FURNITURE WARRANTIES

Although by no means common, furniture warranties are offered by some manufacturers and retailers. Those makers who have them usually offer a one-year warranty on materials and workmanship for case goods and on frames, springs, and mechanisms, if any, of upholstered furniture. Fabric is rarely, if ever, warranted by a manufacturer.

An example of a generous manufacturer's warranty is the one that promises the company will repair or replace defective wood pieces and upholstery frames for five years. Another good warranty offers lifetime repair of outdoor metal furniture frames and finishes and two years for vinyl lace and strapping.

For the purposes of establishing guidelines, here's an example of a warranty program that a full-service furniture retailer was offering recently. It covered defects in workmanship and materials of wood furniture for five years and upholstered furniture frames, springs, and mechanical parts for three years. Fabrics were warranted against wearing out and fading for one year. After that year, the firm said it would recover or replace the fabric at their option for a partial charge. Service calls were free the first year of purchase. After the first year, a service charge would be collected.

QUALITY HOME FURNISHINGS

Quality in home furnishings is a combination of functional operation, good looks, and durability. The fact that poor quality often does not show up until a purchase has aged a bit is a problem, however. A fluffy carpet that looks great new may be subject to excessive shedding and matting, so that in a short time that gorgeous pile has become matted and flat. A shiny surface may become discolored the first time somebody sets a damp glass on it. An upholstered item is a blind item: You can't see what it's made of unless you take it apart—and that's impossible.

 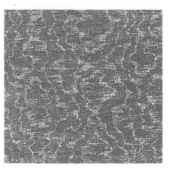 

Some ways to obtain quality merchandise include shopping at reputable places, comparing prices carefully, and reading enough to understand the descriptive terms. Sometimes poor performance in home furnishings is related to an incorrect choice rather than an inherently poor product. Putting a light fabric on a family-room sofa is an example of this type of problem. If you know how to read a furniture tag, it's easier to make appropriate choices.

Wood furniture

Interpreting the information you'll find when shopping for wood furniture requires some knowledge of standard industry terminology. *Solid hardwood* means that each exposed furniture part is made of hardwood lumber. In this construction method, strips or boards are bonded together with adhesives or wood joinery. Unseen parts are not necessarily hardwood. *Hardwood veneers* and *all wood* furniture have veneered surfaces bonded to a reconstituted wood product, such as particleboard, to solid wood or to plywood. Another way to describe furniture of this kind is as *solids and veneers*. Furniture made this way contains some solid wood parts, wood veneers, or artificial laminates and reconstituted wood products.

Artificial wood grain or laminated furniture has a photographically reproduced surface of plastic, foil or paper that is bonded to particleboard or another substrate. When the word *fruitwood* appears, it usually refers to the light brown finish, not to real apple, pear, or cherry. The first two are rarely

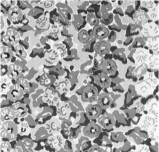

Courtesy of John Widdicomb

used on furniture these days. Since cherry is a premium hardwood, it would likely be identified by name.

When the words *oak finish* or *cherry finish* are used, they pertain to the finish color and grain and do not indicate that the wood itself has been used. Terms such as *solid oak, solid cherry, solid mahogany,* or *solid maple* tell you that this is the wood that has been used to make the furniture's exposed parts. Other types of wood and other materials have almost certainly been used to make interior parts such as drawers, backs, bottoms, and shelves.

The surface of a piece of wood furniture can be either a slab of solid construction or a veneer, which is a thin slice of hardwood applied under pressure to a core of some other wood or composite material. Both methods produce durable furniture. The use of veneers makes possible inlaid or otherwise intricately patterned furniture surfaces of more than one type of wood. Veneers also are used to create a matched pattern wood surface.

Solid wood expands and contracts depending on the amount of moisture in the air; the application of veneers on plywood keeps tabletops from warping and cracking. The existence of veneers means it is possible to have furniture with exotic graining that

would be unavailable or prohibitively expensive in solid wood. High-quality wood veneers are unlikely to separate (*delaminate*) from their substrate. Solid wood surfaces also have their advantages. If they are scratched or nicked, they can be sanded down and refinished; also, they cannot delaminate.

Good methods of construction are certainly at least as important as quality materials. When comparing furniture, use the following guidelines:

Drawers should move freely, yet have automatic stops. Support blocks of wood should be found on drawer bottoms. Interior surfaces should be smooth and free of excess glue. Drawer fronts should be attached with joinery such as dovetail joints, rather than merely butted together. Doors should swing smoothly and quietly and hang evenly, and hardware should be mounted so that it is on straight.

Furniture should be sturdy. Check how easy it is to remove or add table leaves. (Some tables have built-in storage for their leaves—a space-saving advantage.) Does the grain pattern of the leaves match the top, and do the table halves fit together evenly? Check the finish to be sure the surfaces are smooth and free of drips, runs, and bubbles. The stain should be uniform and hard-to-reach areas near joints or carvings should be evenly stained and free of glue.

Storage furniture

Wall systems, modular storage components, and cabinets all hold possessions stylishly. The best choice depends on your budget, what you want to store, whether you might be moving soon, and the style of your decor.

There are two decorating choices for storage units: keep them as background, unobtrusively blended with the room's architecture, or match them to the rest of the furniture. If money is tight or you are planning to move, modular units could be the best solution because they usually blend in with the background and are easily moved to another location.

Since a wall system is a very large unit, chances are good that it will become the focal point in any room in which it is installed, so make sure it can stand up to all that attention. Although they began as contemporary furniture, wall systems and modular storage units (individual components that can be used alone or combined to form a storage system) now are available with traditional decorative touches, such as dark finishes and architectural moldings.

■

Modular storage units can blend into the background.

If the simple lines of even a traditional wall system seem out of keeping in a period room, individual storage pieces such as cabinets and roll-top and other enclosed desk units can hold a lot while remaining in character with the decor. Tall cabinets with doors can hold television sets, audio and video equipment, clothing, and books, among other items. They also are used to store barware or dishes in the dining room. A storage piece that includes a desk surface as well as space for books and records is an excellent choice in a traditional room where a desk is needed in addition to storage space. The value of an antique piece will be seriously reduced if it is altered, so weigh this course of action before you redo or cut down an old piece of furniture.

Equal in importance to decorating considerations are the durability and strength of storage pieces. They must be adequate to support the weight of the items stored. If the load is light—paperback books, a collection of baskets or knickknacks—you can economize with lightweight shelving. But if heavy audio equipment, hardcover books, or collectibles are to be stashed away or displayed, choose furniture built to bear a greater load.

■

Storage furniture can be an essential part of the decor; this storage wall organizes a large collection of books and periodicals.

© Phillip Ennis

Whether the wall system is assembled at the factory or as a kit, examine the places where tops and bottoms of side panels join. A tight-fitting back panel, cross-bracing, corner blocks, and internal framing are signs of strong furniture. Sturdier pieces are heavier and have thicker shelves. The best assemble-it-yourself systems incorporate carefully engineered, locking hardware, preferably of metal, while in standard furniture, traditional doweled or tenoned joints of wood reinforced with glue are preferred.

A storage system is only as good as its shelves. Moveable shelves are more flexible, but shelves that are structurally locked into the side panels are stronger than the removable type. The shorter a shelf's span, the more densely it can be filled. The rule of thumb is that the longer the shelf, the less weight it can bear per running foot. So, when you need to support a heavy load like books, choose narrow units that have stationary shelves. To be sure of strength, opt for a system with thicker boards.

Since the cost of shelving is related to how much material is used, one money-saving option is to buy the shallowest shelf that will do the job. Standard-size books can be displayed in a bookcase 10 to 12 inches (25 to 30 cm) deep. Art books and stereo components usually need a depth of 15 to 18 inches (38 to 45 cm), and a large television set requires even greater depth.

When shopping for modular storage, you will find two types of units from which to choose: tall units that can be placed next to each other to form walls and stacking units that are individual cabinets of varying dimensions (except for depth). A module can almost always be used either alone or in multiples to form storage walls. Both kinds of wall systems should have some leveling device so that the units used together can be lined up exactly.

In general, stacking systems offer more flexibility than vertical pieces. Since the stacking modules are usually smaller, they can be rearranged in a variety of configurations and built up to different heights. They are also easy to move. It will probably cost more to buy the smaller units since you will need more of them and there is more work involved in making a larger number of complete pieces.

Both kinds of storage usually have special optional fittings to accommodate different storage needs. The most common fittings are doors of glass or wood, drawers, display lights, record dividers, drawers for audio- or videocassettes, and drop-leaf panels for use as a desk or bar. Unless there are pull-out supports for the leaf, consider it a very light duty surface and don't place anything heavy on it. Extra shelves are usually available at added cost. In general, drawers are more expensive than doors and glass doors are more expensive than wood.

Upholstered furniture

Upholstered furniture is a blind item in the sense that the way the piece is made is hidden from view. Ask for information and evaluate the piece on several points: the frame, the springs, the filling, and the fabric covering. Choose a kiln-dried hardwood frame in which the legs are an integral part, unless they are unusual, as with bun feet.

Eight-way hand-tied springs are the traditional mark of good quality. However, you will pay more for this form of construction than for a one-piece unit with zigzag springs, usually known as a Marshall unit. At moderate and lower prices, this type of construction is widely used and is acceptable.

Tradition dictates that down filling is best. But it's the most costly and, unless you like a rumpled look, the most troublesome, since down cushions need to be incessantly plumped after they've been sat upon. A cushion with a polyurethane foam core wrapped with Dacron polyester is easier to care for and less expensive. Avoid shredded foam seating since after a time it will mat and become lumpy.

If the furniture has to stand up to heavy casual use, choose a tightly woven fabric that has a factory-applied soil-resistant treatment. Be aware that the fabric grade and its durability are not necessarily related. Grade measures the cost of the fabric, which is governed by the fiber used and time

needed to produce it. Many durable fabrics are inexpensive. Nylon and olefin, for example, are long-wearing fibers used in many low-cost fabrics. Blends frequently combine the best characteristics of two fibers. All fabrics will fade in direct sunlight.

Sofa beds, recliners, and modular seating are among the most useful upholstered furniture you can buy. Their multiple uses make them especially valuable in small spaces where one piece must serve several purposes. As with any multipurpose item, be sure to test for all functions. For example, first sit on a sofa bed to judge its comfort as a sofa. Then open it out into a bed and try it. Compare several brands of sofa beds to see which is easiest to open and close.

Courtesy of Pier 1 Imports/room design by Samuel Botero

■ *OPPOSITE PAGE:*
Be sure that the shelving you select is sturdy enough to hold what you're planning to store. Hardcover books are quite heavy and need strong shelves.

■ *LEFT:*
A mix of patterns for throw pillows is one of the most decorative treatments you can choose for upholstered furniture.

Wicker furniture

Traditionally used to furnish porches and conservatories, both old wicker and reproductions are increasingly being used in every room of the house. Wicker's charms include informality and moderate cost, and it works particularly well in country interiors. Popular spots for wicker today, besides porches and protected outdoor settings, are bedrooms, family rooms, hallways, and living rooms. New all-weather wicker, which has been treated with special chemical finishes, can be left outdoors even in unprotected places.

Wicker is a weaving process rather than a particular kind of material, and wicker furniture can be made of any number of fibers. The technique of wrapping coarse fibers loosely around a furniture frame dates back to early Egypt, and over the ages, many different fibers have been pressed into service. Today, however, willow, buri (or Philippine palm), and rattan are frequently employed.

Styles available include both the fanciful late-Victorian curlicued excesses and plainer old pieces popular in the late nineteenth and early twentieth centuries. Tropically inspired pieces usually come in brown, tan, and natural rattan. Contemporary-style woven rattan pieces in dark, jewel-like tones, such as ruby and emerald, and in pastels are a fairly recent innovation; the pastel-toned seating has found special favor in subtropical climates.

When selecting new wicker furniture, keep the following points in mind: The tighter the weave (regardless of style or material), the more durable and long-lasting the piece is likely to be. If the furniture has been painted, inspect it carefully for uniformity of finish. Two coats of semigloss latex enamel paint are considered necessary. If in a natural finish, it should have been sprayed with a clear lacquer to prolong its life and simplify maintenance. Run your hand over the piece. It should be smoothly finished to keep from snagging clothing and bare skin.

The Chinese Cheung style of woven rattan, which features a very tightly woven seat and back, offers extra durability. Any piece should feel sturdy and comfortable with no wobbling.

Many people select seat cushions for wicker furniture that comes without them. Shop for these add-on cushions at the same time as you buy the seating to ensure a proper fit.

Take the following steps to maintain and preserve wicker furniture:

Prevent dust buildup and wipe the piece down occasionally with a cloth dampened with water and a mild household cleaner. Glossy rattan in a brown finish can be cleaned with lemon oil.

If tiny nicks or scratches occur in a glossy dark surface, touch them up with one of the commercial products available for this use.

Buri pieces should not be polished or waxed under normal circumstances, so find out at time of purchase whether your furniture is made of buri.

Unlacquered furniture that will receive heavy use can be sprayed with a clear varnish to seal the surface if this has not been done already.

To touch up painted wicker, make sure the area is dry and dust-free. Prime the bare spots, then use a spray paint on the spot. Cardboard makes a good backdrop to prevent paint from going where you don't want it.

To tighten loose wrapping on furniture, gently unwrap a few turns of the rattan peel and lightly spread glue on the frame. Then rewind the area tightly and use tape to hold it in place until the glue dries.

■ *RIGHT AND OPPOSITE PAGE:*
Outdoor furniture of cast
or wrought aluminum
offers outstanding quali-
ties of durability and
resistance to rust.

Outdoor furniture

Most people want outdoor furniture that lasts a long time, requires minimal maintenance, is lightweight enough to move around easily, yet not so slight that it topples whenever it gets windy. Those with little storage space appreciate furniture that is durable enough to stay outdoors year-round or that stacks so it can be stored in a small space. Stylish outdoor pieces, especially in wood and metal, can often function just as attractively indoors.

Besides wood and wrought iron, you'll find aluminum and plastic (known as resin, or PVC) furniture for outdoors. Within each type of material, there is a rather wide set of options in prices, styles, and colors. Aluminum and plastic furniture are the most popular types of outdoor furniture, but wood and wrought iron are gaining popularity.

No outdoor furniture can continue to look beautiful without maintenance of some kind, so find out how to care for your new furniture when you buy it. Look for tags with information or ask for guidance from the retailer.

Although styles change only slowly, changes in color are noticed every few years. Presently there's a trend to maintain harmony with nature rather than to use strong contrasts. Colors such as leaf green and rose pink are popular. Still, you'll be keeping the furniture for quite a few years, so ignore fashion and choose what you really love. It's sensible to coordinate furniture color and style with the color of the house or trim. If the outdoor area is directly off a kitchen or family room, another choice is to coordinate with the colors and design of the indoor area.

Most dealers assume you want to buy a dining table, umbrella, and four or six dining chairs. This is a fine choice for those whose primary interest is dining furniture. But for many people several comfortable lounge seats and a coffee table or side table will be more useful. Whatever you choose, authorities say opting for better quality and therefore longer-lasting pieces produces greater economy than buying the least expensive pieces you can find and then having to replace them.

Courtesy of Brown Jordan

Aluminum furniture doesn't rust, so it can withstand the salty ocean air. It is usually relatively lightweight, so it can be moved fairly easily. Aluminum pieces can be made of extrusions or tubular forms that are bent and welded, or they can be made in molds in a more expensive process known as casting. Cast-aluminum pieces often duplicate the look of wrought iron. Popular these days are cast-aluminum reproductions of Victorian and Regency pieces formerly made in wrought iron.

The newer powder-coat finishes come in many colors and textures. Some aluminum frames come in mottled or antique looks such as verdigris or bronze. Other styles combine two or more colors. At lower cost, anodizing is a durable protective coating.

▪
By selecting an all-weather mesh seat, you minimize the problem of protecting against the weather.

Courtesy of Brown Jordan

Aluminum furniture requires relatively little maintenance. Wash the furniture with a garden hose several times a season and plan on an application of automotive wax at the beginning or end of the season. The cushions or vinyl strapping used on aluminum or on any type of outdoor furniture need to be washed regularly too. Rain does not count as washing, since rain brings with it airborne dirt.

Prices for aluminum range from low, for inexpensive tubular chairs, to high, for a top-of-the-line cast-aluminum dining set consisting of a table and four chairs. Up to a certain point, as you know, you get what you pay for.

Plastic furniture that is made of polyvinyl chloride can be extruded and molded. When it is extruded into tubular or pipelike forms and cut and assembled into furniture, it is usually called PVC. When molded, the same material is known as resin furniture. A piece can be made from a single-injection molding or assembled out of molded parts. It doesn't sound like all of this would make for attractive furniture, but it does. Read on.

The material requires little maintenance (hosing down, typically) and holds up well over a long period. A factory-applied coating on PVC furniture extends its good looks by protecting the material from the ultraviolet rays of the sun, which over several seasons can turn uncoated resin furniture a dingy yellowish color.

Plastic furniture is light and easy to stack. However, the lightest pieces can be knocked over by a moderately strong wind. They remain cool to the touch, even in hot sun; and salt air and salt water don't affect them. The rounded, egglike look of molded resin furniture is an appealing and unusual style. There is a wide range of prices.

Wrought iron

These days wrought-iron furniture is made of cold-rolled steel rather than iron. Among the most appealing pieces are the lacy Victorian styles that are, if anything, even more popular for indoor use. Although there are aluminum copies of this ornate furniture, steel is the material of choice because it can be machined into thinner bolder shapes.

Care and maintenance is costly for wrought iron since it will rust once the finish breaks down. However, you can delay rusting indefinitely by touching up scratches as they occur. The available number of finishes and colors has been increased in recent years; some popular new looks imitate very successfully the look of aged materials: bronze, verdigris, pewter, and simulated rust and marble.

Wrought-iron furniture is moderate to high in the price category. At lower prices, you might get chairs with expanded wire mesh seats. At higher prices, you'd be more apt to find distinctive, hand-plaited seats and better cushions.

Wood

After being out of favor for a decade, wood furniture is enjoying a comeback, especially in classic reproductions of English Regency, Mission, Arts and Crafts, and Adirondack styles. Teak and cypress as well as redwood, oak, ash, and pine are among the available woods. These are often treated with preservatives and coated to keep them looking good.

High-quality wood furniture is far from cheap. In expensive pieces, check to see if exposed hardware is brass. If not, it may rust. A nice feature on more costly sets are wood plugs that cover the hardware. Beware of the painted reddish furniture, which many people refer to as redwood and which has lost popularity recently. For one thing, it is not necessarily made of that durable and long-lasting wood; it may simply be stained with a redwood finish.

Though bulky, heavy, and potentially difficult to store, wood furniture can be left outdoors in all weather. It should be cleaned regularly. Wood furniture that reproduces styles found in late-nineteenth- and early twentieth-century England is available in fine garden shops.

■

Rustic wood furniture is once again quite stylish.

Part Two
THE ELEMENTS OF A ROOM

Introduction

IF YOU WERE to analyze all the interiors of buildings in the world, you would discover that the most beautiful and functional ones conform to innate concepts of proportion, scale, balance, and harmony. The best effects are achieved through the manipulation of lines and masses or shapes that have particular textures and colors.

Perfecting a knowledge of the complexities of design elements—including line, form, texture, balance, scale, and proportion—to create interesting and comfortable rooms is the lifework of designers. Those who embark on a decorating project can benefit from the awareness that there is a theoretical basis for success. Good decorators break rules, and so can you; but we all willingly obey the laws of scale and proportion because they are built into our perceptions. In fact, obeying aesthetic rules is something most people do naturally. Being aware of these principles doesn't limit your creativity; it may help you figure out what's wrong when a first try at a decorating scheme doesn't seem to work. Some principles that you'll discover and be influenced by are scale, balance, and harmony.

Scale

Scale refers to the overall relationship between a room's measurements and its furnishings. People can be comfortable in both large spaces and small ones. Using scale well, however, usually requires consistency. It's not only that small spaces often look best if the furniture is in keeping with the size of the room, but also that selections should work together to conform to the spirit that is created.

A fair amount of delicate furniture in a small room makes perfect sense. A lesser amount of somewhat larger pieces also is workable. A very large piece like a grand piano or king-size bed presents a problem in a small room, but not in a larger room. One big piece chosen carefully can add an element of surprise or even fool the eye into seeing more space than is really there. But a small room crammed with large pieces will make most people feel uncomfortable.

Up to a point, you can counteract the effects of mismatched scale between a room and its furnishings. If the furniture is too slight and small to be spread out over the entire area, section off the room with a divider (potted plants, bookcases, or a paneled screen) and arrange the furniture in part of it. Use the rest of the room for something else. If the furniture is massive but the room is small, put some of the pieces in storage or in another room. A wall of bookshelves can be made less imposing by leaving some of them unfilled. Add a few plants or art objects for visual interest.

Balance

Draw an imaginary vertical line down the middle of a room to establish its center. People generally feel more comfortable if both sides are in visual balance. They don't have to match exactly, but if almost all the furniture were in one half of a room and the other half were almost bare, the room would look odd.

Balance in a room can be even and symmetrical or uneven and asymmetrical. In the latter case, though of different sizes, the furnishings in an asymmetrical room are of similar visual weight. Most rooms are primarily asymmetrical in balance, and strictly symmetrical arrangements are static and therefore somewhat boring.

All things being equal, a large shape has more visual weight than a small one. But things are usually not equal, so it's possible to make objects of different sizes achieve balance. A small, dark, irregular or textured shape is equal to a larger, lighter shape.

Rhythm

Repeating forms, colors, shapes, and lines sets up a kind of rhythm that energizes a room design. Let's say you install an interesting wallpaper border of sea shells around a room at slightly above eye level. Then you find a fabric that pictures one of the shells in a different size and cover an ottoman with it.

■
Breaking the rules can produce remarkable results. This small room has been given a strong treatment to good effect.

You've employed rhythm to enliven the room. The key to rhythm is a continuity that comes from organized recurring or developing patterns. Like an overly coordinated outfit, however, too much rhythm (and too many shells) can be intrusive or silly.

Harmony

A harmonious room is one with consistency in scale and mood and the vitality that comes from a bit of variety. There are enough ways to arrive at harmony that you need not worry that it is an unattainable destination. If on a first try, the room's "music" isn't as sweet as you'd like, keep some of the melody and add some new notes.

THE GEOMETRY OF DECORATING

Reduced to its basics, a room and most of its furnishings are nothing more than geometric shapes. Doors, windows, beds, sofas, and tables are rectangles, squares, or triangles that run the gamut from pencil-thin slivers to fat cubes. Add circles to your repertoire and there is literally nothing you can't do with design. A knowledge of geometry can help you employ all these forms in more interesting ways.

Vertical lines, for example, appear to resist gravity and therefore are energizing. Horizontal lines tend to be restful. The eye registers short and interrupted horizontals as lively dashes. A long horizontal rectangle has the restful quality that we associate with lying down on a bed. A standing vertical, like a standing body, is a livelier shape, attached firmly to the ground yet ready to move around.

Triangles, indeed all diagonals, are dynamic and create an impression of motion, whether they are the long oblique lines of a sofa or bed set in the middle of the room at an angle instead of against the wall or the small interrupted lines in a fabric with a pattern of triangles. Chairs set at an angle enhance conversation between the people who are sitting in them.

The use of diagonals also creates an illusion of more space than is actually there. A sloped ceiling directs the eye toward the wide-open spaces near the ceiling. Expansive diagonal arrangements of furniture not only feed the illusion but also look jewel-like and important set in the middle of the room with plenty of space all around them.

Curved shapes such as circles, cones, cylinders, and spheres bring variety into a static interior. Circular forms remind us of all that is living—the bodies of people and animals and the forms of flowers, fruit, and vegetables. When a room seems to be tight and constricted, introduce a round table or rug, a round ottoman or chair, round cushions or vases, or even fabric with circles on it.

Big upward curves are often experienced as uplifting and inspiring. Horizontal curves suggest gentle and relaxed movement. Large downward curves bring a sense of solidity and attachment to the earth. Small curves suggest playfulness and humor.

In the chapters that follow in this section, you will be introduced to basic concepts for all decorating projects and all room schemes, regardless of period or style. We will investigate the principles of color, lighting, how to treat walls, ceilings, and floors, fabric selection, and windows. Finally, we'll consider choosing and arranging accessories for a room.

■ *OPPOSITE PAGE:*
Curved shapes bring vitality into a room setting, as this unusual set shows.

Chapter 1

COLOR

IT HAS BEEN observed that some colors clash in juxtaposition while other colors blend together in a more pleasant harmony. However, there seem to be almost as many prescriptions for choosing a good color scheme as there are colors. Some authorities suggest opening your closet to see which colors you enjoy wearing and then duplicating them in your home. One expert advises taking a trip to the supermarket to buy fruits and vegetables, then bringing them home to ''play'' with until you come up with a mix you like. Another ploy is to key a room's colors to an important work of art that will be displayed there.

Each of these ideas has merit, especially if you are starting from scratch. But finding colors you'd like to live with is merely the first hurdle. Deciding how much of each to use and which tints or shades to select is the heart of the matter.

Although there are myriad workable color schemes, there are some problems that almost always arise. Many amateurs select too many colors for one room, producing a chaotic atmosphere. Or they may choose a very intense color—say, fire-engine red—and use it in such a large area that it becomes tiresome and more of an eyesore after a while. Often, seeking to avoid the problem of using too much color, people eschew bright colors altogether and opt for safe neutrals. This results in dull, lifeless rooms.

You don't have to become familiar with the color wheel or the names of the different types of color schemes in order to choose colors that work. If you don't want to master the technical aspect of color, follow this simple tip: Select something with at least three colors (not including white or black) that you like and can use in the room. It could be an area rug, a decorative object, a painting, or a fabric. Select the quietest hue as your major color; choose a brighter color as an important accent and the brightest color to be a smaller accent.

For a more academic approach to color, and one that will probably serve you many times in the future, it is worthwhile to learn the definitions of the major types of color schemes. The tool used by artists and designers to make color selections is known as a color wheel. It contains twelve basic colors, which are divided into three primary colors—red, blue, and yellow—three secondary colors—purple, orange, and green—and six tertiary colors—yellow-orange, red-orange, red-purple (or violet), blue-purple (a darker hue of violet), blue-green, and yellow-green.

Black, which is the absence of color, and white, which is the reflection of all the colors, are not considered as colors but are used very effectively with different combinations of the colors on the color wheel.

■

Plastic laminates in luscious colors have brought more color into the kitchen and bathroom.

■

Colorful wallpaper can make an understated room like this one come alive.

© Philip Ennis

■

The oriental theme in this bathroom is highlighted by the use of a simple, though rich, color scheme dominated by red and gold, against a white background.

Other color words you will come across include *hue*, which is simply the name of the color and sometimes is used to refer to a particular tint or shade; *tint*, which is a color to which white has been added; and *shade*, which is a color to which black has been added.

Saturation is a term that refers to the depth or intensity of a color. A very brilliant and intense color is known as highly saturated.

Planned color schemes can be classed into a number of types, some of which are easier for an amateur to execute.

Monochromatic schemes use a single color in a variety of hues. An example would be a room in various shades of blue.

Monotone schemes are a variation in which neutrals of the same tone predominate.

Analogous or *adjacent* schemes use hues that are next to each other on the color wheel. Two exam-

ples are blue with blue-green and blue-violet or green with blue-green and yellow-green.

Complementary schemes employ hues from opposite sides of the color wheel: red with green, orange with blue, and yellow with violet. These bright and balanced schemes are usually very popular. The biggest danger is that they may be too bright, like flags and sports costumes. Safeguard against this by choosing a quiet hue for one of the colors and covering large areas with it.

You can also work with three hues that are equidistant on the color wheel. An example is red, yellow, and blue. Some schemes employ four hues spaced around the wheel. Both of these are somewhat more difficult to execute since they are more complex. The easiest color schemes to work with are harmonious ones that include monochromatic and analogous combinations. Both are safe because they avoid clashes.

Texture, pattern, and shine affect the appearance of colors, and placement of one color in relation to the others also plays a role. For example, light colors appear lighter when they are seen against a dark background. Dark colors become darker against a light background. A medium tone can be made to seem either light or dark through its contrast with its surroundings.

Warm colors advance and appear closer; cool colors seem to recede. Placing sharply contrasting colors together can cause an unusual sense of vibration. You can use these optical illusions to make small spaces seem larger and to render oddly shaped rooms a little less noticeable. A long and narrow room, for example, will seem less narrow if the front and back walls are painted a strong, warm color while the side walls are painted a light, cool color. The front and back walls will appear to come closer while the sides will seem to move away. A dark ceiling will tend to seem lower than the same ceiling painted in a light tone. A dark floor and ceiling can greatly reduce apparent height if you so desire. Painting a door the same color as a wall will cause it to blend into the room; painting it a different color will make it stand out.

A single color can unify a space. Lighter colors enlarge and dark colors minimize. Brilliant color can become a focal point and deep, vibrant color can heighten dramatic effects, especially under artificial lights. The warm midtones on the color wheel (reddish pink and peachy orange) are flattering to many people and are easy to live with.

Studies of human response to color have established that lack of color variety creates boredom while too much variety and contrast exposes people to sensory overstimulation. The studies show that too much of one color, such as tan walls, beige upholstery, and a brown rug, can lead to restlessness, irritation, and difficulty in concentrating. At the other extreme, exposure to bright colors—say, a loud plaid sofa, shiny red wall covering, and a black-and-white rug—can cause similar adverse reactions in people.

■
Warm peach colors are flattering to many complexions.

© Jennifer Levy

Being aware of these color effects can help you choose a color scheme that not only appeals to your senses but also minimizes flaws and creates the desired atmosphere, which could be calm and restful, dignified, stimulating, or exciting.

In general, designers suggest selecting the dominant colors first. These are the hues that will occupy the largest spaces: floors, walls, and ceilings. Then consider secondary areas such as furniture, window treatments, and accessories. Add small areas of color in strong values as accents in the form of throw cushions and artwork.

In order to judge how or whether a scheme will work, collect samples of possible fabrics and finishes and mount them on a sample board in the same size relationship as in the contemplated room. The sample board should include swatches of material, samples of paint colors, and other furnishings. Even more useful is a watercolor or colored-pencil rendering of your room. Designers routinely create such helpful tools, and do-it-yourselfers with the talent and interest can do the same.

COLOR AND GEOGRAPHIC VARIATIONS

There's often a subtle variation in favorite colors from one geographic region to another. Although certain popular colors cross borders, the particular shade or tint of the popular hue varies according to the natural landscape and quality of light in that particular area.

The colors of New England in the northeastern United States and eastern Canada include cranberry red, deep green, and earthy browns. The same colors in tones of the American Midwest are persimmon red, khaki green, and pumpkin. In the tropical South, these colors are lighter—pearlescent ivory, honey yellow, and moss green. On the West Coast, where the sun is at its strongest, colors are the most brilliant—vivid yellow, turquoise, bright orange, and spring green.

Color surveys for the 1990s predict that warmer colors will predominate: More yellows, deeper reds,

Courtesy of Benjamin Moore & Company

■ *OPPOSITE PAGE:*
The red of the lively, floral wallpaper in this bathroom creates a warm, inviting atmosphere.

■ *LEFT:*
The tender green tones of this bedroom ensemble are incredibly soothing; they aptly reflect and highlight the quiet and beauty of the seaside setting.

browns, and greens, and colors associated with Native Americans and with tribal, ethnic influences from all over the world, including Asia and Africa, will be popular.

The geographic locale and orientation of the windows give a room a natural aspect that can be warm or cool. Color can help to strengthen or correct the exposure, depending on your needs and the impression you wish to create. For example, if natural light is inadequate, you can use lighter colors to take advantage of what light there is.

Decorators often ask their clients whether they will be using the room mostly during the day or mostly at night. If the latter, they will present a scheme using colors that don't require sunlight to look great. Pastel colors usually look best in the light of day; they tend to fade into drabness when the sun goes down and you have to turn on artificial lighting. However, by using a full-spectrum light source, you can minimize the nighttime drawbacks of clear garden pastels.

It's generally accepted that the living room and dining area are used at night for entertaining, so their colors should look good under artificial lights.

The aspect of using color to hide dirt and stains comes into play in childrens' rooms, hallways, kitchens, and any area that gets heavy use or is exposed to soot and airborne dirt particles. Darker colors or multicolor patterns can hide dirt and flaws more effectively than light hues.

■*RIGHT:*

To visually enlarge space, select a light color scheme in which white predominates.

Courtesy of Brooks Rogers, Inc.

Despite the fact that the human eye can discern at least ten million colors from an infinite spectrum (as Sir Isaac Newton discovered in the seventeenth century), many people are confused about how to combine colors for a satisfying decorating scheme.

"Most people are either trendies or traditionalists," says Margaret Walch, a director of the Color Association of the U.S., a color forecasting group. Those who are extremely receptive to new color ideas are considered "trendies." A trendy would have advocated the use of postmodern colors or faddish tropical pastels or perhaps would have preferred high-tech black, white, and red long before these color trends became widespread. Traditionalists would be more likely to have stayed within a Victorian or a Southwestern palette, favoring mauve and rose mixed with pink and traditional blue shades such as periwinkle, navy, and sky blue.

Instead of looking at what others are doing, consider your own color preferences. One reason for examining the items you buy and wear is that people often have erroneous ideas of their own preferences, says Walch. "They may say they love traditional things; but they don't have any of the accoutrements."

Well-designed rooms usually center on a dominant color or family of tones. Too many contrasts give a disorganized impression. Of course, decorating rules are made to be broken, but novices are safer using the brightest colors sparingly. The smaller the form, the more intense the color can be. A coherent color scheme can blend furnishings of different periods and styles.

Color proportions are as important as the colors you choose. A gray room with a hot red accent is quite a different place from a red room touched with gray, even though both rooms technically have the same color scheme.

Unless you want them to stand out, the larger objects in the room, such as sofas, draperies, and cabinetry, should be in restrained colors. Choose colors in keeping with a room's purpose. Enliven an entry with bold color, but choose a quieter hue for a room such as the kitchen or a bedroom in which you spend a good deal of time.

Color and light

It's difficult to separate the subjects of color and light, since the quality and amount of light greatly affects the impression a color makes. (The subject of lighting will be covered in depth in the next chapter.) Always keep in mind that colors are strongly influenced by natural light that comes in through windows and by artificial lighting. That's why you must look at fabric swatches, rug samples, and color chips in the room in which they will be used or at least under the type of light that will be present. A swatch seen under fluorescent light will look different from the same swatch under incandescent light.

■*OPPOSITE PAGE:*

The pristine beauty of a pure white color scheme endears it to many minimalists.

Decorators' Pointers on Color

■ Use color to rearrange space. Monochromatic schemes can camouflage decorating problems such as columns or pipes. Play up an architectural strong point like a fireplace or a window bay by painting it a different hue (say, two shades lighter or darker) from the rest of the room.

■ As the average home gets smaller, people must learn to live in more modest spaces, which often have little in the way of architectural interest. Visually expand a room with light tones, or a small overall-pattern wall covering. Strong, aggressive tones make a room seem smaller and cozier.

■ A small room doesn't have to be white, says New York interior designer Bunny Williams. Paint the room a soft salmon and the woodwork creamy white for spaciousness without boredom. "Light colors make you less aware of those low ceilings that are the norm in today's housing market," she says.

■ Select the same solid color for all the floors in a house, preferably in a light shade, says Sally Sirkin Lewis of Los Angeles. Carpeting makes a room appear larger than if you use several small scatter rugs.

■ Noel Jeffrey uses colorful art to expand apparent space in a small room. "Hang a large mural or a painting that has depth and you are fooled into thinking that you're looking into something; in effect, you are creating another dimension, a larger space," says the New York designer.

■ Lift your color scheme from a favorite painting or lithograph that appears in a room, says Los Angeles–based designer Barbara Brenner. "Splashes of color found in the art become the colors of accessories, pillows, and window treatments. Don't be afraid to be daring with accent colors," she says.

■ If the artwork is both powerful and colorful—an example might be one of David Hockney's or Jackson Pollock's works—decorate in neutral colors to draw attention to the art.

© Phillip Ennis/room design by Barbara Ostrom

COLOR IN PERIOD HOMES

Personal preferences can override correct period color selections, but if you are striving for an accurate representation of a particular style, choose characteristic colors of the era. Each period had its typical colors as well as furnishings. The exteriors of Victorian homes, for example, were often symphonies of five or six carefully chosen colors designed to bring out the details of elaborate architectural trim.

Victorian colors are rich, deep gold, olive, brown, red, and gray. Neoclassical colors of the early nineteenth century were light and clear—for example, sky-bright blue, soft pink terra-cotta, yellow, and cream. In Australia, Federation colors of the early twentieth century were green, yellow, and light brown. A typical modern color scheme might include clear primary colors such as red and yellow against black or, to a lesser extent, white. Postmodern colors such as rose, pink, apricot, and aqua tend to be rather dusty or grayed. Another direction you can take for the same period is pastels such as mint green and baby blue. Southwestern colors take their hue from the sun-baked desert—earthy browns and reds and sandy beiges mixed with the blue of a semitropical sky.

■*ABOVE:*
Gold tones and dark paneling enhance period decor.

■*OPPOSITE PAGE:*
Primary colors and strong contrasts are typical in modern schemes.

■

These deeply saturated reds and blues make for a sophisticated room highly suited to nighttime entertaining.

Bright colors on older buildings are very popular now. The fashion for colorful houses started in San Francisco in the 1970s and now has moved all over the country, according to Elizabeth Pomada and Michael Larsen, whose 1978 book *Painted Ladies* documented the beginnings of the interest in multi-hue paint jobs on residences.

"The color movement isn't funded or directed by anyone. It has grown because people love the look of the painted houses," says Pomada. Paint, which has saved many old structures by making them look better and increasing their worth, has even played a role in the revival of such towns as Cape May, New Jersey, Port Townsend, Washington, and Ferndale, California.

In Bridgeton, New Jersey, for example, historic painting led to a housing renewal in one community. Beginning in 1983, the small coastal town about an hour north of Cape May began giving free paint to low-income residents of deteriorating nineteenth-century homes. By 1990, several hundred homes had been painted as people began to see their old houses as charming antiques instead of white elephants. The paint jobs had gotten owners interested in making repairs to roofs and furnaces, too, so the housing stock was upgraded on several levels.

"The cheapest thing you can do to upgrade a single house, a whole block, or a town is to paint it. Paint is what gives historic districts continuity, and many communities are adopting color guidelines," says Roger Moss, an American historian whose specialty is nineteenth-century American design.

While brightly colored houses were creating visual excitement in the 1970s, scholarly research was disclosing that paint colors in the nineteenth century were actually far brighter than had originally been supposed. In this day and age, there are two schools of thought on color in period houses: Some people prefer to select historically authentic colors while others please themselves without regard to history.

As a historian, however, Moss says that the so-called historic colors marketed by paint companies are not necessarily accurate. Often, there are more authentic colors in their regular lines, says Moss, who found acceptable substitutes for thirty-four old paint colors by comparing the old and new paint charts of the American paint companies, Sherwin-Williams, Benjamin Moore, Glidden, and Devoe. There are also likely to be many other paint lines with appropriate colors. Guidance on the right color can come from books on specific periods, house museums, and paint charts put out by paint companies at your local paint store.

"You don't have to pay for special paints or hire an expert to get an authentic paint scheme," says Moss. "You just have to know a bit about historic colors, and if you do minimum research, you will find that out."

The Decorating Life

The colorful blue and mauve exterior paint scheme is the icing on the cake for Bob Hover of Troy, Michigan, who spent ten years rescuing an 1888 house from demolition and turning it into a comfortable home. He used three shades of blue and two of the reddish-brown mauve from a paint company's historic Victorian color line.

Hover removed many layers of paint in the renovation of his home and even considered a chemical analysis in an effort to learn what the house's original color was but found it was too expensive. Earlier coats of blue, violet, and one startling bright yellow had all blended together by the time he began removing them by hand-sanding.

After sanding down to bare wood, he chose oil-based paints for his home. He applied three coats of a top-grade paint, a white prime coat as a base, a second prime coat in blue and a third coat of finish paint. Although oil-based paint is harder to work with than water-based, he thought it would last longer. (This point of view is disputed by some paint manufacturers.)

He had satin-finish and semigloss formulations mixed half and half at the paint store to get the degree of shine he wanted. He estimated that it took twenty to thirty gallons (75 to 115l) of paint to cover the house with three coats. Working evenings and weekends, it took him two years to paint the exterior.

The difficult, protracted, and detail-oriented work that goes into a project of this scope may seem daunting, but the rewards of such an undertaking are equally immense. There is a magnificent feeling you get from living in a house that you have restored and decorated yourself.

Courtesy of Bob Hover

Courtesy of Bob Hover

▪ *Bob Hover was able to recreate the feeling of his Victorian house even though the color is different from the original. He chose a color scheme that combines three shades of blue and two of a reddish-brown color.*

Chapter 2

LIGHTING

■
Brilliant lighting turns this enclosed outdoor space into an island of light at night.

SINCE LIGHTING NEEDS fluctuate depending on the task at hand and the amount of available daylight, flexibility is one of the most important attributes of a lighting system. Although people tend to focus on what the fixture looks like, its placement and the quality of light it emits also have an effect on decor.

The light source can alter the appearance of colors, patterns, and textures of fabric and surfaces, and its placement controls the kind of shadows it casts. Learn more about lighting in a practical way by experimenting with the location of your lamps and by observing the effects when you vary bulb wattage.

There are three lighting functions that need to be considered in every room: *background* or *general* lighting for the entire room; *task lighting,* which provides a pool of light needed to perform specific tasks such as reading, desk work, hobbies, and food preparation; and *decorative lighting,* which contributes to both mood and style. Examples of decorative lighting are a chandelier over the dining table or a neon light sculpture mounted on the wall of a family room. Decorative lighting, of course, also adds to the room's general light level and may contribute to task lighting needs.

A rule of thumb for every room is to provide at least two of the three types of lighting. Dimmers allow you to adjust lighting, and several different light sources make it possible to turn an ordinary space into a dramatic one, conveying a variety of moods in the same room.

To show how attitudes toward lighting have changed, consider a hypothetical dining room of the past and present. Formerly, a ceiling-mounted fixture above the table would most likely have been considered adequate. A demonstration of desirable dining room lighting in a New York showroom recently required six different kinds of fixtures. There were wall sconces, picture and plant lights, wall washers, accent lights and a chandelier.

Installing so˙ many light sources is more costly than using one overhead fixture, but it is far more interesting. And there really is no other way to achieve a sophisticated lighting system.

You can, however, improve your existing lighting at a moderate cost. Place all or most of the lights on dimmers. This relatively simple step expands a system's flexibility by permitting variation in the intensity of the light in a room. Dimmers come in a great range of prices. While high-quality dimmers will do their work silently and for a long time, the least expensive dimmers tend to hum when turned on and to break down in a shorter time.

Besides dimmer controls, low-voltage lights offer the advantages of less heat, greater economy of operation, and smaller fixtures. The beam of light is fairly intense, so it's best as an accent rather than task lighting.

Another option for more dramatic lighting is to employ color filters that snap on to many low-voltage fixtures to create light with a blue, red, green, yellow, or orange cast. Blue-filtered light intensifies the brilliance of silverware and crystal and also creates interesting effects when placed behind plants. The other colors are used primarily for creating a fun atmosphere. Using different colored filters, it's possible to create a light show on your wall and thus employ colored light in place of artwork, if you so desire.

When shopping for lighting, take swatches of fabric and paint chips along since different kinds of lights can change the apparent look of the colors. The combinations are endless.

■

There are many different types of light switch; choose one that matches its surroundings.

Courtesy of Lightolier Controls

Courtesy of Lightolier Controls

AN INDOOR LIGHTING PLAN

How much light is enough? That depends on a number of factors. Rooms with dark walls and appointments tend to absorb light while rooms with light colors reflect it, so you may need more lighting sources in darker rooms.

If you are building or remodeling, you should have a written lighting plan on which all the functional and decorative lighting is indicated so the wiring can be installed where it is needed. Plan switch locations to allow a walk through the house from lighted area to lighted area without having to go back to turn off a light. Make sure you have outlets in the hall and foyer where you might need them for lamps and to run appliances such as a vacuum cleaner.

Place controls in easily reachable locations. Note areas where extra lighting would be convenient, such as in showers, closets, and stairwells.

Lamps and shades

Short of adding new lighting, you can give a room a lift by adding a lamp or two in character with the rest of the room's decor. Advances in technology such as halogen bulbs and low-voltage lighting have encouraged a greater flow of contemporary designs. For traditional interiors, lamps with authentic period detailing are becoming more sophisticated and more widely available. Since lighting was available in the late nineteenth and early twentieth century, having lamps and fixtures that are in character adds considerably to the room's effect.

The high cost of period originals by famous early designers such as Louis C. Tiffany, Emile Galle, Gustav Stickley, Dirk Van Erp, and Frank Lloyd Wright puts them out of reach of most people. Reproductions, however, are more affordable.

There is a fairly good supply of authentic turn-of-the-century light fixtures and lamps. Electrified oil lamps with glass shades, chandeliers in brass and crystal, floor lamps, and table lamps can be found in specialty shops, auctions, estate sales, and, if you are lucky, flea markets. Typically, the pieces need

© Phillip Ennis

new wiring and socket replacements, and if brass, they require refinishing.

New shades are less expensive than new lamps, yet almost as effective in making a change for the better. Over the years shades tend to become dusty, dirty, frayed, and shabby, so new ones can brighten a room more than might be supposed.

■

Choose a light shade that maximizes the amount of light from your lamps.

▪

Firelight, candles, ceiling-mounted fixtures, and lamps all work together to create pools of light in this room.

▪*RIGHT:*
Under-cabinet lighting provides essential task lighting while ceiling-mounted downlights provide general illumination.

▪*OPPOSITE PAGE:*
This light fixture provides indirect lighting with a modern accent.

© Jennifer Levy

Courtesy of William K. Schoenfisch

Before selecting a new shade for a lamp, bring the lamp into the shade store and try several different sizes and shapes. As a rule, the less variation between top and bottom and the more neutral the color, the more traditional a shade will appear. By choosing a traditional shade material, such as string or parchment, in an extreme shape or an unusual color instead of white or beige, you can change the look of the lamp from traditional to trendy.

Shades should be deep enough to hide the bulb, wide enough to spread the light, and dense enough to obscure the light bulb. Shades lined with white will reflect the greatest amount of light. Shades can be translucent or opaque. Light spread is more noticeable with opaque shades because of contrast.

If a lamp is providing light for reading or tasks make sure the shade is wide at the bottom. The wider the opening, the wider the beam of light will be. If a large area is to be illuminated by light that reflects into the room from the ceiling, choose a shade that is wide at the top.

A table lamp next to seating requires a shade whose bottom is at eye level. Plan on placing a table lamp with a shade above eye level behind the seating. Lamps with a shade above a person's head should have a light diffuser to avoid having light shine in the eyes.

Re-covering a shade is simpler than picking out a new shape. Many lamp outlets will re-cover shades using the existing framework. Handy types can re-cover a shade themselves. Look in home sewing pattern books to find how-to information. When re-covering, make sure to measure both the height of the table on which the lamp will sit and the seating height.

Lighting the kitchen and bathroom

The typical kitchen often lacks lighting at counter level, where it's most needed, and can therefore be greatly improved if under-cabinet lights are installed. Place these under-cabinet lights toward the front of the cabinet so that the complete counter is illuminated. If you place them too far back, the front part of the counter may fall outside the pool of light. Since much food preparation takes place over the kitchen sink, be sure to provide adequate light above the sink.

There is the choice between incandescent and fluorescent under-cabinet lighting fixtures. If you choose fluorescent lights, opt for soft white bulbs since standard fluorescent light is uncomfortably harsh.

In the bathroom, avoid placing the face in shadows by positioning lights at the sides as well as on top of the mirror over the sink. If it's impossible to place a light on all three sides, it's better to eliminate the top light and keep the two side lights.

Track lighting

Since track lighting comes in many configurations and lengths, it's one of the most flexible tools available for bringing light to an entire room without worrying about whether there's an outlet handy. Installing track lighting is usually the most economical solution to the common problem of an inade-

■ *OPPOSITE PAGE:*
Lighting can be functional and decorative at the same time. These bare bulbs surrounding a generous mirror offer the best of both worlds.

quately fixtured older house or apartment without enough outlets.

Depending on the type of bulb and housing you select, you can produce a sufficient level of general illumination, bathe an entire wall in light, aim a strong and controlled beam of light to highlight an object or painting, or illuminate a desktop or counter for a specific task. Lighting effects depend partially on the type of bulb chosen and partially on the location selected for the fixture. A single track can accommodate a variety of different bulbs. Light sources can usually be easily snapped in and out, so the track can be refitted if lighting requirements change.

For accent lighting of objects on shelves along a wall in a room with an 8-foot (2.4-m) ceiling, mount a track 18 to 24 inches (45 to 60 cm) out from the wall on the ceiling. Use a single fixture to highlight each object. To wash the same wall with light, place the track 24 to 48 inches (60 to 120 cm) away from the wall. If the track is 24 inches (60 cm) from the wall, place fixtures at 24-inch (60-cm) intervals. You can also mount track on a wall vertically or horizontally. Usually, a knowledgeable lighting retailer can suggest appropriate equipment and locations if you describe what you are trying to do.

When selecting fixtures for the track, be aware that lamps that look similar may still generate different beam spreads and intensity of light and color. Several basic types of fixtures are available to help you create a variety of effects. *Floodlights* in a fixture reveal an area in much the same way as it is revealed during the day. *Spotlights* dramatize one portion of the space or object in a group. *Backlighting* an object creates a silhouette of it on the wall. Shadows are by-products of light and can be elongated or heightened depending on the position of the light source. Experiment at night by placing a light in different locations near a group of houseplants and observing how the shadows change.

The addition of a rheostat, or dimmer switch, to a track-lighting setup will give you even greater flexibility in choosing a particular intensity of light. This is a minor installation that has a major impact.

Halogen lighting

Halogen lamps, light bulbs, and fixtures are a fairly new ingredient in lighting products. Halogen light produces an intense, clear light that shows colors in true tones, making it an excellent medium for artworks, general illumination, and, with precautions against glare, task lighting.

The drawbacks associated with halogen bulbs include greater heat and higher prices. Since halogen bulbs offer about 2,000 hours of light, retaining consistent light output throughout life, compared to about 1,000 hours of light for incandescent bulbs, their higher initial cost is made up in longer life.

Their intense heat and the fact that halogen bulbs contain gases under pressure call for some safety precautions. Don't put a halogen bulb into a fixture with a plastic socket. The bulb itself should be shielded so it doesn't come in contact with another material. Keep halogen lamps and fixtures away from curtains, bedspreads, and other fabrics that could catch fire from the heat of the bulb. Never touch a bare halogen bulb with your fingers or hand. Body oils deposited on the bulb's quartz exterior can create heat sinks that cause lamps to fail prematurely. A cloth should be used to dust or replace a halogen bulb. Some halogen bulbs have a double casing—a good safety feature.

Fluorescent lighting

Cool to the touch and economical because of its long life, fluorescent lighting is usually preferred in industrial settings where economy is a central concern. It can offer the same benefits at home.

A drawback to using fluorescent light at home in a room where incandescent bulbs are also used is that fluorescent bulbs cast a cool bluish aura compared to incandescent light, which has a warm, somewhat yellow cast. To avoid this problem, choose a color-corrected fluorescent bulb that produces a glow similar to incandescent bulbs. Warm white and warm white deluxe fluorescent bulbs can eliminate that telltale bluish cast and make fluorescent lighting more appealing in the home.

Courtesy of Lightolier

■*LEFT:*
A chandelier is one of the most dramatic types of lighting fixture you can select for a dining room.

LIGHTING PERIOD HOMES

The problem with installing lighting that could never have actually been used in a period room is that it subtly undermines the room's character. Sometimes the period of the fixture is correct, but it would not have been used in a particular way. Chandeliers, for example, are frequently hung in entryways of Colonial-style homes. Yet they would not have been put in an entryway since their candles would have blown out when the door was opened. A frequent mistake is placing period fixtures so high up that the interesting details are lost. Most homes today have levels of general illumination that are far brighter than in the past.

Except where safety requires that a fixture be at a higher level—for example, on a stairway—strong lighting is almost always out of place in a period home, says Roger Moss, author of *Lighting For Historic Buildings*, a book that describes how American homes were lit. Moss advises that dimmers be used on lamps to supply a lot of light when needed and a lower, more comfortable and attractive level for everyday use.

Electrified candlesticks, lanterns, and wall sconces are all suitable for a main room in an American eighteenth-century house, which in its own era was illuminated by candlelight. An authentic treatment might be to place sconces at either side of a mirror. Mirrors were very practical in the eighteenth century because their shiny surfaces intensified the small amount of available artificial light by reflecting it.

People either did without light altogether or carried a candle into the bedroom with them. You can stay in tune by eliminating the ceiling fixture and installing wall sconces instead. Simple unobtrusive bedside lamps will accommodate your need for light without clashing badly with the room's decor.

As the nineteenth century progressed, oil lamps became more common. Electrified oil lamps available in reproduction and as originals and lighting fixtures based on Neoclassical design themes are appropriate in rooms of the early nineteenth century.

Kerosene lamps, lanterns, wall sconces, and chandeliers were important lighting sources in homes in the latter part of the nineteenth century. In some parts of the United States kerosene was used well into the twentieth century, since many areas were without electrification until the 1930s, when the Rural Electrification Administration was set up by President Franklin D. Roosevelt.

Electricity was available for city houses beginning in the late nineteenth century—New York City, for example, was electrified in the 1890s. At first, electrical service was not very reliable. As a result, lights that could operate on either gas or electricity were popular at the turn of the century and both original antiques and copies of these lighting fixtures are now fairly common.

The early-twentieth-century bungalow with its attic dormer and large front porch was usually electrified. Antique lamps and fixtures are quite costly these days; however, reproductions of Arts and Crafts–style lighting are coming on the market.

Early electric lamps and fixtures were lit with carbon filament bulbs, whose quality of light is softer than the light from today's tungsten bulbs. An American company, Kyp-Go of St. Charles, Illinois, makes and sells carbon filament bulbs. Among the company's products is an exact copy of a bulb made by Thomas Edison in the 1890s. Historic restorations and film producers are among those who order the carbon bulbs regularly. Carbon bulbs screw into the same type of socket as tungsten filament bulbs. (Write to Kyp-Go for a free catalog of old-time bulbs: 20 N. 17th St., St. Charles, Illinois 60174; 312-584-8181.)

■*OPPOSITE PAGE:*
The more light sources you have, the more dramatic your lighting can be. Wall sconces and ceiling fixtures are enhanced by shiny walls and even by the reflective surface of the glass in picture frames.

AN OUTDOOR LIGHTING PLAN

Observe two basic principles in lighting your home grounds. First, plan lighting so it coincides with the intended uses of the landscape. Second, plan lighting and plantings together. In a new outdoor area when most plantings will be small, choose a few larger shrubs and trees to light. Later, as the rest of the garden becomes established, you can add more lighting. You can "sculpt" effects by selecting certain aspects of the landscape for illumination. You can choose not to light unattractive areas.

Illuminate paths and outdoor seating areas that will be used at night. Light flower gardens or other natural features. Don't light areas that will not be used. Or if you do, for safety or other reasons, make sure that the various lights are on different switches so that they can be turned on or off, according to need.

Outdoor lighting extends the use of the outdoor areas by making them accessible at night, promotes safety and protects your property by discouraging intruders, and adds to the sense of visual space from within the house. It can be used to set a scene as lovely as any painting, which you can observe from the window.

Try to avoid merely floodlighting your outdoor living area. Floodlights are flat and offer few contrasts. You need interesting shadows to bring the landscape to life. Reaction to outdoor lighting is largely conditioned by the level of brightness. Subdued light is experienced as more relaxing. But the level of light will have to be intensified to be viewed from a lighted room or patio. To avoid creating reflective glare in window glass at night, put both indoor and outdoor lighting on a dimmer. By varying the levels of illumination, you can create many moods.

A lighting engineer can judge how a landscape will look at night simply by viewing it in the daytime. But for beginners, it is not so easy. Those with little or no experience with landscape illumination will have to do things the hard way. You can take a 100-watt bulb on an extension cord around the landscape at night, placing it in various locations

■
Through judicious placement of light fixtures you can emphasize particular features of your outdoor landscape, during the day or at night.

and then observing the effects. In this way, an inexperienced individual can discover the best method of lighting the garden.

Lighting the outdoor areas that can be seen from your windows will enhance the interior of your home by producing an exterior vista and thus eliminating the black hole that uncovered windows produce at night.

Light the patio or terrace just outside your window so that some sort of continuity is maintained with the inside floor. That way, there is no sense that the terrace is floating in space. You should also provide a vertical edge to the outdoor space you have created with light by installing a fixture that illuminates a wall, shrub, or tree at the edge of the terrace. A sense of an outdoor room is the effect you are striving for.

If you would like to illuminate the house itself, place one or two fixtures from 2 to 3 feet (60 to 90 cm) away from the building and turn the light source toward the building. The light will show the house, revealing the texture of the wall and perhaps also illuminating a flower bed or shrub by the entrance.

All exterior lighting fixtures should be moisture-proof and weather-tight so they will be unaffected by rain, snow, mud, dust, or extremes of temperatures. The fixtures should be of a noncorroding material as well.

Though we usually expect our lights to stay put, sometimes it makes sense to shift lighting, perhaps on a seasonal basis. If you expect to move your light fixtures, choose portable low-voltage systems with spike-mounted lights. Often the lights can be installed by simply sticking them into the ground on the spike, so they can be moved easily to another location.

Low-voltage bulbs are less expensive to operate and safer since the electric current is substantially reduced. The light quality can be experienced as softer and more flattering to garden, terrace, and people, too.

Many low-voltage lighting systems come with 100 feet (30m) of wiring and a single transformer that supports all the fixtures in the system. Usually, six fixtures can be located along the 100-foot (30-m) length. There is a wide choice of individual fixtures, including spotlights to illuminate a specific plant or object, twinklers that can be reflected in a pool, nonglare floodlights for overall lighting, uplights and downlights, overhead lights for parking and activity areas, and mushroom lights that throw a wide beam of light onto a pathway or patio.

You can also buy mercury-vapor bulbs and fixtures, which last much longer and are less expensive to operate than other bulbs, but they have some drawbacks. For one thing, each bulb size needs its own ballast (housing), so you cannot interchange bulbs. The green cast of the light is flattering to foliage but unpleasant on stone, brick, warm-colored flowers, and human complexions.

Where to place outdoor lights

Consider the function you want each light to achieve before you go shopping. It will help narrow choices when you are in a store and facing hundreds of options. When remodeling, evaluate the status of wiring at each outlet. Should it be replaced, or is it adequate to support the fixture you are contemplating buying?

Entrances

Overhead lights, wall lanterns, and downlights are excellent for porches, entryways, and utility areas. Wall lanterns should be placed 66 inches (1.67m) above standing level and can be matched with overhead or over-the-door fixtures.

Walkways

Post lanterns are a signal to visitors that the main entry is being marked. You can choose them to complement entrance lights and to delineate a walkway, driveway, or patio entrance.

Driveways and lawns

Floodlights placed at the corners of the house and garage provide safety and security for large areas. Direct the light beam down at a 45-degree angle to minimize glare. Spotlights and floodlights can overlap or be pointed in opposite directions. Use them to accent special exterior features. Overhead or downlights can illuminate house numbers, steps, back and side porches, and utility storage areas.

Architectural features

Wall-mounted fixtures and floodlights placed near ground level graze and highlight brick and siding details, arches, dormers, and gables.

Maintenance

This should be a consideration when you plan your outdoor lighting system. A common task is changing bulbs in outdoor fixtures. Yet, some fixtures are difficult to open. Or you may inadvertently locate a fixture so that it is inaccessible and therefore difficult to change. Fixtures for hard-to-reach locations should be particularly easy to change. You can cut down on maintenance by selecting long-life bulbs.

If you have low-voltage lights, check them carefully after every moderate to heavy rainfall, since they can easily fall over if the spike loosens in rain-soaked earth. At the beginning of the season, check any outdoor lighting system to make sure it is operating properly and to tighten any connections that may have loosened. Then do the same thing at the end of the season.

■
For safety's sake, make sure that all paths are well-lit.

Chapter 3

A ROOM'S SURFACES

■ *OPPOSITE PAGE:*
After walls, the floor consumes the greatest area. A patterned carpet can give this substantial area added emphasis.

■ *RIGHT:*
Both the brick pattern of the floor of this room and the inviting rug get added emphasis from the interesting baskets on the floor.

IF A ROOM'S surfaces are interesting, it will be an interesting room, regardless of how much (or how little) money has been spent on the furniture, asserts English decorator Kevin McCloud.

This authoritative point of view shared by many decorators runs counter to the beginner's ploy of painting the walls and ceilings white and covering the floors with a neutral carpet. If your furnishings are spectacular, a low-key approach to surfaces may indeed be the best course. But it's often more feasible for the surfaces to provide the excitement that dramatizes fairly ordinary furniture and accessories. Let's consider some of the more lively things you can do with the surfaces of a room.

No matter what choices you make on surfacing materials and treatments, you should first consider the following points about every material:

■ Original and long-term costs of the product
■ Appropriateness to the decorative scheme
■ Durability of the material
■ Difficulties of repair, change, or removal.

© Phillip Ennis

WALLS AND CEILINGS

A little creativity can make any of the common wall and ceiling treatments, which include paint, wallpaper, fabric, paneling, or mirrors, special. Instead of simply wallpapering or painting and being done with it, you could combine treatments by painting the walls and then applying a wallpaper border near the ceiling, at a midpoint on the wall around chair height, at the baseboards, or as an outline for windows and doorways. You might mirror one wall or use wood paneling as a background against which you place open shelves for books and knickknacks.

Paint

Paint is the most common choice for walls and can transform a room with color. Furthermore, paint is usually the least costly option. Improvements in custom blending at the retail level make it easier to get an accurate match even if the sample is one of those traditional stumpers—a silk scarf, a flower petal, or a leaf. The store computer also makes it possible to match exactly a chip of paint from an existing wall that has darkened over time so that you can touch up the wall without completely repainting the room.

Do-it-yourselfers are often advised to stick to water-based paint since it's easier to apply and dries faster than oil-based paint. Recent changes in latex paint formulas have resulted in improvements in color and gloss retention. Unlike oil-based paints—also known as alkyds—they are quick-drying (they dry in about a half hour), so you can put on two coats in one day. Furthermore, once dry, latex is easier to touch up than alkyd.

An eggshell-finish paint has the low lustre of a flat and the washability of a semigloss. This formulation is recommended for children's rooms, bathrooms, kitchens, and high-traffic areas. If you are painting a wall a dark color like hunter green, an eggshell finish is recommended because it will not readily show rub marks or grease marks.

You can get guidance from paint retailers on how to prepare wall surfaces, the best type of paint for the job, the amount to buy, and application tips to make the job go smoother. A dealer can tell you, for example, that new plaster requires a different primer than old plaster or sheetrock.

The upper and lower limits of paint prices encompass a wide range, but buying high-quality paint is always in your best interest. The lowest-priced paint may give two to three years of service, while a better-quality paint will last for seven or eight years. The top-priced paint may, if all the conditions are right, last even longer. Better paint usually goes on smoother and covers better. Since the price of the paint is usually the smallest part of the cost of the paint job if you are hiring a professional, too much economy is penny-wise and pound-foolish. To save money and still get good service, buy more expensive paint on sale.

Specialty paints can alleviate maintenance problems. Some paints have fungicides that resist mildew. Others have been formulated to resist moisture and blistering. Damp-proofing masonry paints and coatings are useful for concrete block or masonry walls or floors, especially if water has already stained the masonry. You can use a clear waterproof coating to protect brick and concrete driveways from the effects of the salt and calcium chloride in snow-melting compounds. This type of coating will also protect brick from efflorescence or peeling due to frost.

If you should decide to paint a bathtub, shower stall, or an area where water is likely to stand on the surface, choose a catalyzed epoxy paint, a two-stage application that is waterproof. Since epoxy is abrasion-resistant, it would be a good choice for a garage or playroom floor, too. Graffiti-resistant coatings are similar to masonry sealers. They are such hard coatings that they don't allow writing to penetrate and you can then wipe or wash it off.

Nonslip paints contain sand that gives them a gritty surface. Then there are the rust-inhibiting paints that are ideal on outdoor metal furniture. There are also special primers. Aluminum paint can be used on radiators to inhibit rust and permit greater heat emission.

Recently interest has grown in *faux* (meaning "false" in French) finishes, which are paint applications that simulate other materials such as stone or plaster or create an impression of age. Faux finishes have two main advantages: They are interesting to look at and they disguise bad walls. Some common faux or painted finishing techniques include glazing, antiquing, wood distressing and graining, and marbleizing, all of which can be learned from books that describe the techniques.

Applying special effects definitely requires more skill and effort than conventional painting, especially such techniques as wood graining and marble-

■*LEFT:*

If you are lucky enough to have an architectural feature of distinction such as crown moldings, emphasize them with a special surface treatment.

izing. Some easier techniques include color washing, gilding, crackle varnishing, and wood distressing. Color washing adds both color and an arresting texture to walls.

■*LEFT:*

A trompe l'oeil wall of books is a surface treatment of distinction.

■*OPPOSITE PAGE:*

Add visual height by placing a decorative border at the very top of the wall.

©Melabee Miller/Envision

Courtesy of Connie Beale Inc

■ *ABOVE, LEFT:*
A wallpaper border treatment is an effective finishing touch for a wall.

■ *ABOVE, RIGHT:*
Use the border to reinforce some aspect of the room. In this case, the delicate border is in keeping with the understated nature of the room.

Trompe l'oeil, which in French means "fool the eye," is a decorative treatment in which you use paint to simulate three-dimensional pictures. Flowers, garden scenes, and animals may be painted on a portion of a wall. One of the most famous examples of *trompe l'oeil* painting is the so-called treaty or map room of nineteenth-century English households in which an entire tiny room is painted to look as if it were totally covered with treaties or maps. (The popularity of the look has led to the introduction of wallpapers that mimic painted *trompe l'oeil* effects.)

A stencil is a paper cutout pattern or template that is placed against a wall, floor, or a piece of cloth and painted in. Typically, a single cutout pattern is moved along the wall so that a linear pattern results. Stenciled borders usually are applied around doors or windows or near ceilings or baseboards and can be in any room of your choice. More complexity results when several patterns are used to create a design.

The usual stenciled design is a small repeat, very often of a floral or architectural motif. Traditionally a feature of country-style rooms that are decorated simply and at small expense, the same technique can be used to achieve unusual effects by applying a large design in a random fashion. Artist Althea Wilson stenciled a 14-foot (4-m) dragon on a bedroom wall, for example, and it became the main decorative motif in the room.

Dividing a wall into several different areas is a traditional nineteenth-century treatment.

Changing a motif's size is simpler when you have access to a photocopy machine that enlarges images. Enlarge an interesting pattern in a book and use it on a wall or a fabric that can be made into curtains and upholstery, changing a room totally with the new designs. A stencil design can be made more interesting if you set it against a surface with a textured paint finish, such as color washing, or wood graining. Bare plaster walls also make an unusual background. Stencils sprayed in gold or silver paint will add luster to a decorative scheme.

Use precut stencils (available at paint outlets) and special stenciling paints, which are thicker than other types of paint and won't run, to succeed with this highly decorative technique.

Wallpaper

English floral, country check, big or small scale, vinyl, grasscloth, shiny or matte finish: There are so many choices in wall coverings that narrowing down a pattern can be by far the most difficult part of the job. It's tricky to know which design will work best on your walls. While large patterns generally go with big spaces and small patterns go with small spaces, there are exceptions. You might want a big effect in a tiny vestibule; achieve it with an intensely bright paper or a giant pattern.

Use the following guidelines to reduce the confusion. First of all, consider the amount of time the room will be in use. If it is a primary room like a master bedroom or a kitchen, choose patterns that

■ *RIGHT:*
*Walls comprise the largest
surface area in any room;
instead of the usual paint
or wallpaper, choose a
more interesting treat-
ment such as this wire-
and-plaster surface.*

■ *OPPOSITE PAGE:*
*Indulge your fancy with
handmade wall cover-
ings, available in stand-
ard and custom colors,
with sculpted surfaces
and hand-rubbed fin-
ishes, and incorporating
a variety of other materials such as sand or fiber.*

are easy to look at and live with. Save bold styles for secondary rooms, such as an extra bathroom or entryways and passageways.

Second, think about the colors that would work in the room. Take into consideration how much sun the room gets. Bold and bright can be harsh in bright sunlight. Strong contrasts are more effective in dimmer light. Don't choose wallpaper for a space until you have observed it at 9 A.M., noon, 3 P.M., and in the evening on both bright and cloudy days. Write down the results of your research in your decorating notebook.

Warm-toned coverings bring the walls in; cool colors provide a sense of expansiveness. Light colors and small prints are unobtrusive while large, splashy prints and shiny metallic papers dramatize space. Small and dark rooms will seem more spacious if you choose pale colors and small patterns. Or create the illusion of a view with a *trompe l'oeil* wallpaper scene on one wall. Lower a ceiling visually by covering it in a bright color or strong pattern.

Consider what is on the walls in adjacent rooms. You can choose a covering in a similar color, with the same pattern scale or the same feeling in mind—for example, a small floral pattern that coordinates with a larger, bolder floral in the same colors.

Many manufacturers these days work with producers of other home furnishings products to develop a coordinated collection of wall coverings and borders, fabrics, and accessories. These are shown and described in attractive room settings in the sample book. Study a selection of the books for ideas.

Select the right type of wall covering to camouflage cracked and peeling walls. A vinyl that is not too shiny and has a small-scale overall pattern will be unobtrusive enough to conceal wall imperfections. Vinyl holds up better in a damp area than paper and works well in kitchens, bathrooms, and children's rooms because it is washable. Solid vinyl on a fabric backing is the most durable; paper-backed vinyl comes next. Vinyl-coated papers are less durable but adequate in bathrooms and kitchen areas that aren't subject to heavy use. Avoid paper in the kitchen because it absorbs grease and shows spots.

Consider textured coverings such as grasscloth, linen, cotton, and silk in formal areas such as the dining room, living room, a study, or home office. The texture adds interest to the walls. Mural wallpapers create a three-dimensional effect that is arresting and can turn a wall into the room's focal point.

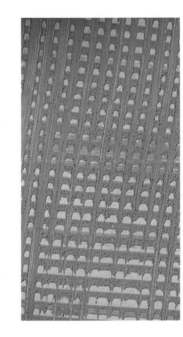

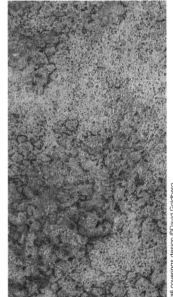

You'll learn just how varied and delightful the selections are when you start browsing through the catalog in a good wall-covering specialty shop. For a small fee you can often order a 3-foot (1-m) square. Take this sample home and tack it up to a wall in the room. Live with it a few days and see if it goes with your furniture, fabrics, and other colors.

Redecorating with wall coverings has become a popular do-it-yourself project. You'll find many shops offering guidance on how to hang the covering and what types of adhesives to use. If you're nervous about tackling the job, consider taking an adult education course to get you started.

If you will be doing it yourself, an important task is to measure a room accurately so you know how much wallpaper to order. A rule of thumb is to measure the distance around the room. Treat doors and windows as if they didn't exist and include the space they occupy in your estimate. Measure the height of the room and then multiply distance by height. Divide the result by 27 to get the number of rolls needed to do the job.

Order all the wallcoverings you need at once so they are all from the same color run. If you buy a roll or two extra, you can probably return it for credit. Ask before you buy. When ordering the wall covering, also buy the adhesives, seam rollers, masking tape, and other required materials. Be sure to follow package instructions and the advice of the professional who sells the materials.

As a safeguard at the beginning of the job, check the lot numbers yourself before unwrapping the rolls; inspect the full length of each roll before you cut it. If there are damaged rolls, return them.

When it's time to apply the wall covering, don't use newspaper to cover the pasting table because the ink may smudge the new covering. Instead, cover it with plain brown wrapping paper or with inexpensive plastic tablecloths or drop cloths.

If you are hanging a new pattern on top of old wallpaper, it's best to strip the old paper from the wall. If, on the other hand, the wallpaper to be covered is in good condition and tight, you can paper over it. It's a much easier task to strip off old

paper if the strippable type or a vinyl covering has been used. Both peel off easily when you grasp a corner and pull. Wash the walls with warm water and scrape off remaining glue with a putty knife after you've done the stripping.

The most difficult situation—wallcovering in bad condition and not strippable—can be dealt with by renting a wallpaper steamer or applying wallpaper remover. Both soften the paper so you can scrape it off with a wide putty knife. After scraping, wash the walls and let them dry before hanging new coverings.

Before tackling a main room with expensive wallpaper, try hanging a medium-weight lining paper in the room. Not only will you get practice in wallpaper application but also the step will improve the final job, especially if you are covering a problem wall. If leaks or mildew has been a problem before, spray an antibacterial agent on the pasted side of the wallpaper before hanging it.

For a better-looking job, work slowly and don't try to finish the project in one day. Wallpaper paste dries slowly enough so that you can adjust a strip and eliminate seam mismatches and bubbles if necessary.

Save extra wallpaper since you can put it to many uses. Most importantly, you can fix small tears and loose edges without repapering. For loose seams, apply paste to both the wall and the wallpaper. Press the paper in place and smooth it with a seam roller. Then wipe away the extra paste.

To patch a small damaged area, paste a new piece of wall covering larger than the tear over the damaged areas, matching the pattern exactly. Allow the patch to set but not dry entirely. Then cut through both areas. Clean the now-empty area, repasting the top piece. Wait fifteen minutes and roll the edges smooth.

What else can you do with leftover wallpaper? Cut out some of the motifs and apply them to lamp shades and accessories. Wallpaper a closet. Create custom waste receptacles—large, round ice cream cartons are often free for the asking from ice cream stores. You can also paper plastic or metal wastepa-

■

Save extra wallpaper in case you need it for repairs, especially in a bathroom or kitchen.

98

A wooden ceiling and floor work together to create a strong impression of rural luxury.

■ *OPPOSITE PAGE:*
Drape damaged walls with fabric and nobody will ever know what's underneath.

per cans. Build a folding screen with pine boards and hinges and wallpaper the boards. Use wallpaper inserts on kitchen cabinets, bathroom countertops, and picture frames. Wallpaper borders can be used to update and enliven old furniture; all you have to do is glue them on. You can also use leftover wallpaper to wrap gifts.

Other wall and ceiling choices

Covering one or more walls with fabric can be a good idea, especially if the walls are in bad shape. Fabric also serves as a sound and heat insulator and looks new longer than wallpaper. You can glue, nail, or staple fabric directly to the wall or use a track system to hang it. The latter method has the advantage of not damaging the walls or, if they are very

bad, saving you from having to deal with them. A good deal of extra fabric is needed if you wish to create soft folds, known as shirring. Patterned flat sheets are a good source of moderately priced fabric. When working with sheets, however, carefully match them to make sure that the grain runs true. Do-it-yourselfers in the past have discovered variations in pattern and color that give a sheet-covered wall an amateurish look.

Another covering for walls is wood or imitation wood paneling. The range of styles and prices for wood paneling is substantial. At the high end is veneered paneling of costly woods like walnut, rosewood, and teak. At the low end is photographically reproduced wood. When shopping, make sure to see the material rather than a picture of it. Paneling can be applied vertically, horizontally, or diagonally.

Wall Pointers

■ Use wallpaper borders in unexpected places such as along the top of baseboards or around door or window frames. They create an impression similar to moldings at lower cost and with less effort.

■ Paint baseboards a different color from the walls or give them a special finish, such as marbleizing. To create the impression of crown molding, paint stripes.

■ Bad walls? Cover them with fabric. A simple system is to make grommets in the fabric, top and bottom. Attach a line of hooks or nails to the wall on firring strips. Then hang the fabric from the fasteners. Use canvas or fabric remnants or sheets.

■ Use soft-white fluorescent strip lights to encircle a section of a room with a perimeter of light. Install the fixtures on top of cabinets or conceal them with a molding strip.

Tiles are sometimes used to panel a portion of a wall, especially in kitchens, bathrooms and entryways. Choices include ceramic, metallic, cork, and mirror tiles. Acoustic tiles are used for ceilings, especially where it's advantageous to absorb sound and when a dropped ceiling is desirable.

Putting mirrors on one or more walls can visually expand the apparent size of a room that is too small or the depth of a room that is too narrow. Reflecting mirrors make the most of available natural light. Mirrors used as a background impart an interesting character to whatever is set in front of them, whether it is a wall cabinet, console table, or lattice or other decorative molding.

An entire mirrored room, such as a small guest bathroom or foyer, is one of the most dramatic spaces imaginable. However, mirroring walls is both a costly and a difficult installation best left to professionals. A mirror that is not lying absolutely flat will create odd reflections and give visitors the impression they've wandered into a carnival funhouse. Mirror installers should take wall irregularities into account when measuring.

Safety is also important. Never rely on glue to hold up a mirror. Glue deteriorates with age, and if it allows the mirror to fall, there could be a serious accident. Shatterproof mirror is a worthwhile option, although it adds to the cost of the installation.

■

If you need to replace or cover a bad ceiling on a budget, consider synthetics that may also offer acoustic properties.

FLOORS

Floor care is one of those domestic tasks that recurs endlessly. Since it will account for much of the time that goes into home maintenance, practicality and easy care in flooring are as important as decorating and budget considerations. The initial high cost of better grades of carpeting, wood parquet, ceramic and vinyl tiles, and sheet goods usually can be justified because of their greater durability and easier maintenance.

Always factor the room's intended use into your decision on floors. Areas like kitchens, bathrooms, entryways, and laundry rooms, which are subject to moisture and potential spills of fluids containing chemicals, should be covered with easy-to-clean flooring that can withstand frequent soaking.

■
A checkerboard pattern is one of the strongest decorative devices for a floor, especially if there is a strong contrast between the two colors and textures of the pattern.

Soft-surface flooring

Area rugs, floor mats, and carpeting are known collectively as soft-surface flooring. The great decorative advantage of carpeting is the unity it imparts to the home. Especially in a small place, wall-to-wall carpeting provides a greater sense of space. A good general rule to follow in small homes is to stay with the same color carpet from room to room. Textures can, of course, be varied. Where two different colors or textures meet at doorways, it is a good idea to put a metal threshold strip or a wood saddle between the two.

Carpeting is among the more expensive treatments, therefore, if you are in a temporary space, it's usually not the most economical, unless you have to hide very bad floors or you need the insulation. Both carpets and rugs come in a variety of fibers and quality levels. Quality affects both durability and attractiveness. Whereas wool remains the top-rated choice, it is also the most expensive. Man-made fibers—especially nylon—have been greatly improved in recent years, providing lower-cost options that still give excellent wear and are very attractive.

■

A good rule of thumb is to make other surfaces unobtrusive if you have a strong surface treatment such as a colorful rug.

© Philip Enns

The most frequently mentioned problem with soft-surface flooring is the need to protect it from spots and stains and the inevitable difficulties associated with removing them. Nowadays, carpet with improved stain-resistance properties is available to minimize this drawback. A key to successful maintenance of carpet of any fiber is to remove stains immediately after they happen. Frequent vacuuming to take away surface dirt is also very important. Pay special attention to edges and to the area that gets the heaviest use—for example, the carpet directly in front of the sofa. Spot cleaning should be done frequently, and you should periodically have carpets professionally cleaned. If you do it yourself, follow the manufacturer's directions.

Area rugs can define a seating area, create an atmosphere of coziness in a large room, and effectively create zones in rooms. Unless the rug is unusually large, most people will walk around rather than over it, so it marks off a conversation or activity area quite nicely.

The styles, textures, and shapes that area rugs are available in are numerous. Choices encompass all the traditional rug types and enlarge on them with contemporary designs. Area rugs can be put down on top of carpet as well as on bare floors. They provide splashes of color on a neutral floor. It's not necessary that all the rugs in a room be the same pattern. Different kinds of rugs that relate to one another in color and feeling can work together without clashing.

Though this is far from an exhaustive list of all the types of area rugs available, some of the most likely choices are orientals, dhurries and kilims, needlepoint rugs, folk-art rugs, and contemporary rugs.

Orientals are said to be the most popular type of area rug. So various are their styles and colors that a good match can be found for almost any type of room—modern, period, formal, or informal. An added advantage is that a fine-quality rug may appreciate in value over the years.

Dhurries and kilims are both flat-weave rugs, usually with intricate patterns. Dhurries originated in India and often come in pastel colors that look wonderful in subtropical climates. Kilims originated in Asia Minor and are known for their rich, deep colors. Although of ancient lineage, they add life to understated contemporary rooms.

Needlepoint rugs that at one time were primarily made in Portugal are now exported from many other countries as well. The handmade rugs can be made to order with almost any motif. Folk-art rugs are examples of folk art extended to rugs. Countries with characteristic folk-art rugs include Poland, Romania, Mexico, Peru, Norway, and Denmark. Native American rugs are part of the folk-art tradition. Contemporary rugs run the gamut from expensive, custom-made works of art to low-cost abstract prints in synthetic fibers.

Sources for unusual rugs include art and craft galleries, craft shows, and antiques shops, as well as the standard rug specialty and department stores.

■

The choice in area-rug patterns ranges from cartoon characters to oriental rug patterns.

■ *Horizontal patterns naturally create an impression of greater width.*

Floor pointers

Give bare wood and concrete floors a painted faux border of marquetry and a painted medallion in the center. Coat the floor with polyurethane to make it durable. Take the designs from old books and antique pieces of furniture.

Bordered carpet runners look better on stairs. You can achieve a low-cost border effect with a striped painted border at each side.

Hard-surface flooring

Choices include ceramic and quarry tile, brick, marble, wood, vinyl, terrazzo, and slate. Tile is an easy care, long-lasting surface with generally good resistance to abrasion, water absorption, chemicals, dirt, and fire.

Since tiles vary to some extent in terms of durability, consider the characteristics of a particular tile in relation to the location. If the floor is likely to be walked on while it is wet, choose tiles with a very low water absorption rate that provide traction. Some tiles have an abrasive grit added to the surface to minimize someone's chances of slipping when the floor is wet. Water absorption rates range from near zero for fully vitrified stoneware to 25 percent for majolica.

Tile grouts can be an important design element. Both color and width will affect the overall look. Dark-colored grouts are recommended for floors, since light-colored ones will darken with use. A matching grout will blend into the tile for a unified look. A contrasting grout will emphasize the grid or pattern formed by the tiles. The wider the grout, the more accentuated the pattern will be. Though grouts come in fewer colors than tiles, it's possible to mix grouts to get a color that will blend well with the tile.

When you are selecting a tile pattern for floors or walls, always remember that the size of the tile should generally be kept in proportion to the size of the room you are selecing for. A large room may easily take a 12-inch (30-cm) tile while a smaller room calls for a smaller tile.

Floor tile shapes can be used in combination. An attractive mix is white octagons with small black insets. Or create a border by laying a perimeter of rectangles end to end and then fill in with square tiles or a pattern. Rectangles can be arranged in a single or double herringbone formation, staggered or used to create another design. Squares can be laid on the diagonal or in a brick pattern. You can combine different colors and patterns to give the illusion of an area rug. Another design idea is to use wood strips to frame tiles.

The decorating life

There is no single "right" answer to many decorating questions. It's a matter of making choices.

■ *Should I replace the braid rug in the living room?*
NO: The room is acceptable as is.
YES: It's a bad color for the room; it's soiled and too small.

■ *What should I get instead?*
ORIENTAL RUG?
Pro: Very adaptable to other rooms; long-lasting; requires cleaning and occasional repair but experts are easy to find; portable.
Con: High original cost; I'm not knowledgeable about them; not the best choice for planned contemporary-country theme.

WALL-TO-WALL CARPET?
Pro: Soft, comfortable, especially in winter; good buys available now; will hide discoloration of wood near center of room; satisfactory with decorating scheme.
Con: Not portable; time-consuming for vacuuming and cleaning spills; puppy training could be problem.

STENCILED FLOORCLOTH?
Pro: Free course offered for do-it-yourselfers; hire Mary's friend to do it; in keeping with my decorating theme.
Con: Not long-lasting; not soft underfoot; people could trip.

DECISION
Keep rug, but get it cleaned; ask about dyeing; wait until puppy is trained and reevaluate.
Take class and make floorcloth for foyer; if I like the results, consider having a new floorcloth made for the living room.

Chapter 4

FABRICS

■

Rooms of great complexity in which a variety of patterned fabrics are used call for design expertise.

Courtesy Brunschwig & Fils

Vary textures as well as patterns when working with fabrics.

SOFTNESS IS THE characteristic shared by all types of fabrics, no matter what their fiber makeup, color, or pattern. They can be cut, sewn together, draped, gathered, glued on, tucked in, and generally used to mediate between the hard edges in the environment and a need for physical and visual comfort. Fabrics are your best friend in any decorating project, since they are more responsive than any other material.

Going back to the beginnings of recorded history, if not further, fabrics have protected human beings from the elements and from hard and sharp surfaces, provided warmth or coolness, and offered visual stimulation and tactile interest. It's safe to say that they are a basic aspect of the concept of shelter.

Recognizing their unique importance on so many levels, most people respond almost instinctively to specific fabrics and their combinations of texture, pattern, and color; falling in love with some and strongly disliking others is a natural part of the design process.

In decorating, fabrics are a primary resource used to improve any room. They are one of the easiest, least expensive, and least intrusive ways to vary an environment. Selecting fabrics can and should be a joy rather than a chore, particularly since the breadth of choice is truly staggering, taking in both natural and synthetic fibers.

There used to be a rather strict hierarchy in which fabrics made of natural fibers like cotton, linen, wool, and silk were accorded a more exalted status than synthetics—nylon, polyester, and olefin. Recent research has focused on improving the performance and appearance of both natural and synthetic fibers. Each fiber imparts specific qualities, and some offer more resistance to soil, have less of a tendency to pill, or can take and hold color better. However, natural properties can be modified or enhanced by various treatments. Chemicals can make a fabric antistatic, fire-retardant, wrinkle-proof, water-repellent, and resistant to damage from fading, dirt, bacteria, mildew, and insects.

Usually there's a trade-off between the advantages and drawbacks of a specific material. Cotton, for example, might feel soft and last for a long time

■

Use the same fabric on walls and windows for a thoroughly coordinated look.

© Daniel Eifert. Design: Mary Meehan Interiors Inc.

but be liable to soil easily. You can compensate for the drawback by choosing a treated cotton and by selecting a dark and busy pattern that will hide the dirt.

Color is introduced at one of several points in the process of manufacture: into the fiber itself, into the yarn, or onto the fabric's surface. Some dyes are stronger and more resistant to fading than others. Eventually, however, exposure to the sun and air, and washing or dry cleaning will result in the fading of virtually all fabrics. Make sure you check with the manufacturer for details about the dye.

Here are some general points to be aware of, especially if the fabric will be subjected to hard use and considerable sunlight:

■ Muted colors age better than brilliant and intense colors.
■ Tweeds and diffuse patterns look fresher longer than solid and high-contrast patterns.
■ A nubby or interesting texture can compensate for the gradual loss of color over time.
■ The availability of the fabric is important; you may need to replace it some day.

■

A single floral fabric covering all surfaces can be successful. However, make sure that it's really the fabric you want before you employ it so lavishly.

■

The successful use of fabrics involves careful selection of texture as well as color; many fabrics that you use in a room will be felt as much as seen.

Weaving, knitting, knotting, twisting, tufting, and felting are the methods of fashioning fabrics. Most home furnishings fabrics are woven. Printing is accomplished mechanically and by hand with wood blocks, screens, and wax and dyes in techniques such as batik and tie-dyeing. A pattern can come from the way the fabric is put together or from surface printing or from both. Fabrics also can be ornamented or embellished through stitchery, as in embroidery, appliqué, quilting, and needlepoint techniques.

The price of a fabric is related to the costs of the raw materials and the labor needed to produce it. A high price doesn't guarantee that the fabric will be more durable or will be suited to your needs. Low cost doesn't rule out good performance.

Courtesy of Brunchswig & Fils.

Performance and visual appeal, along with budget of course, are the factors that really count when making fabric choices. Overriding physical requirements, such as a need for fire-retardant materials, allergy to a specific fiber, or unusual exposure to the sun also may impose limitations on choice. Other than these requirements, there are few decorating "rules" to be considered other than those of common sense and visual pleasure.

It used to be considered important in decorating to match fabrics to the period or style of room in which they would be used. Denim and damask were treated like pickles and ice cream and never used together. A far more liberal appreciation of the pleasures of contrast has accustomed our eyes to mixtures of formal and informal, ethnic and slick that would have seemed strange only a decade or two ago. Adventurous and talented designers have led the way by breaking the rules and creating great rooms in the process. Their experiments have encouraged others to follow their instincts in fabric selection.

When choosing fabrics, the best procedure is to assemble swatches of all that you plan to use in a room. If you make sure you have samples in the same size relationship as the objects they will eventually cover, you will be able to get an idea of how they will work together. If you love a fabric but fear it will be out of keeping with the rest of the room, use it in limited quantity—for example on throw cushions, as a curtain liner, or a tablecloth.

Reflect as you select that the history, traditions, legends, and technology of turning fibers into fabrics is one of the most glorious stories of human invention. Think of how fabrics have been used as time has unfolded. Oriental rugs, lace, paisley shawls, and tartan are topics that fill libraries with articles and books.

Many people find fabric history compelling. Consequently, there is a rich literature on all aspects of the topic. If it interests you, as it does so many professional designers, writers, and artists, dip into some of the books listed in the resources section of this volume.

© Melabee Miller/Envision

DECORATIVE TRIMMINGS

Once as remote as settings in historical novels, orna-mental decorative fabric trims for furniture, pil-lows, window coverings, and table skirts are being revived. Trims include edgings such as ribbon and gimps that are narrow borders, as well as wide woven and braided borders, fringe, cording, roping and tassels, rosettes and frogs.

Trimmings arose centuries ago to serve a func-tional as well as a decorative purpose. Gimps were used to cover upholsterer's tacks and where the fabric met the molding at the edge of upholstered walls. Cording at the edge of seat cushions made them more durable. It was used with thick fabrics where self-welting would have been impossible.

Elaborate tiebacks held curtains gracefully open. Their ornateness was a reflection of the decorative tastes of the eras in which they originated. These trims are still known by the traditional names and used in the orthodox manner in period rooms. But new uses have been found for them. For example, tiebacks are wrapped around the neck of large Oriental vases so that the tassels hang in graduated lengths. Fluffy fringed tassels are being tied onto decorative keys left in the locks of cabinets and at the ends of lamp chains and window shades.

Heavy braid borders once used on the edge of curtains now are also applied vertically down the center of an upholstered chair. The decoration con-trasts interestingly with a plain fabric covering.

■

Fabric bed curtains once served a purpose before central heating. Now beds are hung with cur-tains purely for decora-tive reasons.

■

Use fabric generously when you want to create a luxurious, Victorian feeling.

Fabric borders are being used at the base of skirts, on decorative pillows, and on swags down the leading edge of a curtain. Twelve-inch-(30-cm-) deep borders make good valances on windows. Wide fabric borders used on the wall add a three-dimensional quality. Slender gimps might decorate a lamp shade or form a monogram on a shower curtain.

Multicolored fringe that picks up three or more colors in a fabric is a finishing detail that can distribute color about a room as well as give a finished look to a pillow, sofa, or chair. Fringe is also used on curtains and to edge window shades. Moss fringe, fine cut, looped, tasseled, netted and tasseled, and corded bullion fringe are a few of the varieties of fringe being used today. There are also fringes with

glass or wood beads. Sheer Austrian curtains edged with heavy beaded fringe offer a contrast between the simplicity of the beautiful curves of the fabric and the ornateness of the trim, which appeals to the nineties sensibility.

To learn how to use trim effectively in a new idiom, leaf through decorating magazines, especially some of the grander publications. Study books that show historical styles. Besides looking at late Victorian styles which made enormous use of trimmings, also consult books on earlier-nineteenth-century Neoclassical styles such as Empire, Federal, and Biedermeier. These styles are more in keeping with today's tastes. Other sources of guidance include window decor shops and fabric showrooms.

▪

The austere elegance of this neoclassical setting is both softened and complemented by generous, flowing drapes.

Chapter 5

WINDOWS

■

When you have a spectacular window, draw attention to it with a dramatic window treatment.

WINDOWS OFFER A view into the world while their coverings protect us from the world's encroachments. Speaking in functional terms, a window's main reason for being is to admit light and air into a residence. Decoratively speaking, windows break up the monotony of walls in much the same way as artworks on the wall by bringing variety to the decorating scheme. They may also enhance by revealing an attractive view to the people living inside as well as to passersby.

How to treat windows is one of the basic decorating questions that should be tackled early in the planning process. The considerations usually center around these points:

- ■ Are the existing windows adequate or are they such a drawback that they need to be replaced?
- ■ Should the windows be a focal point in the room or should they be de-emphasized?
- ■ Should each window be treated separately or would it be better to combine them all in a single unit with a unifying cornice or valance?

Physical deterioration of the glass, frame, or sills, draftiness, and an inconvenient location are just some of the reasons why you might want to consider taking the time to replace old windows. Dark rooms can easily be transformed if larger windows that admit more light are substituted for the inadequate existing openings.

Furthermore, replacing old, inefficient windows with new ones with better thermal properties and low-maintenance frames can net you a more comfortable environment. High-performance glass used in top-of-the-line windows minimizes the loss of heat in winter or coolness in summer due to conduction. So-called low-emissivity glass is coated with a virtually invisible metal that repels the cold and the heat. Other features to look for in new windows include factory-installed weatherstripping and vinyl-clad sashes. Double or triple panes of glass can minimize energy loss and ultimately pay for themselves in energy savings.

New windows can also greatly improve the appearance of your residence from the outside and can turn a shabby place into one with a trim and tidy exterior.

Different types of windows each have advantages and drawbacks. The traditional double-hung window that slides up and down, for example, doesn't get in the way of people or treatments and can be opened top and bottom. This type of window provides little protection from the rain and is hard to clean from the inside.

Horizontal sliding glass windows admit plenty of light and air. Full-length sliders are easy to break and might offer security problems. Half-height sliders can be difficult to reach if furniture is placed beneath them.

© Daniel Eifert . Design: Joseph L. Roman

Casement and awning windows that swing out or in, usually by turning a crank, are easy to open and close and, especially in the case of awning windows, may precisely control the breeze and block the entry of rain. Treatments that slide up and down usually cannot be used with them, however.

Clerestories—horizontal windows high up on the wall—reflect light off the ceiling and cast it into the room. Because the concentration of light is up high, the floor may seem dark by comparison.

■

The spectacular view in this elegant study is highlighted through the use of heavy, generous drapes chosen, for further emphasis, to match the fabric on the chairs.

■ *RIGHT:*
A skylight usually needs some kind of treatment to minimize glare. This treatment can be raised and lowered as circumstances warrant.

■ *OPPOSITE PAGE:*
When you have a solarium, or a window wall, make sure you get advice on how to minimize problems of too much light or the uncomfortable situation of a "black hole" at night.

Skylights can correct problems of too little daylight. If placed properly, a skylight can add considerably more light than a side-wall window of the same size. They are especially effective in bringing light to the top floor, but getting the light from a skylight onto the first floor can be tricky.

Sometimes a skylight admits too much direct sunlight and heat, especially in the summer. To counter the problem, ventilating skylights usually open with a crank handle turned by a pole. Some skylights have a miniblind sandwiched between two panes of glass in a double-pane window. You open and close the blind by moving a wand. A push-button-operated electric motor can control the blind and the window. Terrific—as long as there aren't any power failures.

The shape and placement of windows determine how natural light will enter a room, so consider the implications carefully when selecting replacement windows. Wide windows in the middle of the wall, for example, will provide even illumination. Tall, narrow windows throw light equally on the ceiling and floor, but the opposite wall will not be uniformly brightened.

A window on each of two adjacent walls is likely to provide excellent light penetration, but not if each window is very narrow. The plentiful light that enters through a bay window has a tendency to be concentrated in the bay unless the window is quite tall, so adding a bay window to shed light on the whole room would not work.

Letting the outdoors into the house is a contemporary concept. In bygone times, when insulation was poor or nonexistent, and people chopped wood to keep warm, there was considerably less interest in the view from the windows. A change in heating methods may help explain the popularity of adding one or more window walls to a room. A window wall offers easy access to the outdoors, reveals a great view, and floods a room with light.

It also creates glare, minimizes privacy, exposes occupants to potential excess heat or drafts, removes a length of wall from use, leads to greater color fading; and unless it is covered or the exterior is lighted, a window is a black hole at night. Look at each of these issues in turn and consider how you will solve the problems that they raise.

Glare is a consideration not only with window walls but with smaller openings as well. One way to reduce glare from windows is to minimize the contrast between the window and the wall. If you have a window that admits plenty of bright sunlight for a good part of the day, choose a light color for the walls of that room rather than a dark color.

Many rooms have several single windows that are not the same size but should all have the same treatments. Start planning with the largest or most difficult. Then treat the others in a scaled-down version of the first.

A skinny single window need not look like a lonely soldier on sentry duty. To give it more visual weight, hang draperies well on the wall to either side. To make a squat window seem taller, install a cornice or valance above the window so the bottom of the cornice is level with the top of the window.

■

*Ideally, a distinctive
window such as this
should be left uncovered.*

To hide a small, oddly shaped, or inappropriately placed window, match the covering to the color of the wall and window frame. A simple shade in the same color will seem to disappear into the wall.

There are a number of ways to turn the windows into the focal point of a room. Give them importance by framing them with paint. Paint the window trim and sills in a color that contrasts with the surrounding walls.

If the windows don't have much trim, add some with ready-made decorative moldings to create the three-dimensional relief effect of a picture frame. Choose molding in a style that is appropriate to the room decor and architecture. Ask yourself what type of picture frames would be appropriate in the room and use something similar as window trim. In a room with Oriental accents, for example, use a fretwork molding that is a classic Chinese Chippendale design detail. In a country house with natural wood trim around the room, accentuate the area around the window with the same type of wood moldings.

Sometimes it seems that a wall with a window is removed from use as surface against which to place furniture. But this doesn't have to be true, especially when the window extends only part of the way down the wall. You could create a window seat to be carpeted or cushioned. If you don't need a seat but do need storage space, build in a bookcase beneath a window and then carry out the idea by building bookshelves to surround the window as well.

When you want to emphasize the view, have your covering clear the window by drawing back beside it. Curtains and vertical blinds are especially useful in this situation. Or select a treatment that rises above the window glass. Shades or venetian blinds fill the bill. You could also choose a sheer covering that reveals the view but still offers screening for privacy and some glare control.

If windows are to stand out and attract the eye, contrast the treatment with the walls or place an interesting piece of furniture or accessory between two windows.

Special situations
No windows
Rooms below ground level and apartments often present no opportunity for adding windows. If a room has a closed-in feeling because it lacks windows, you can paint a *trompe l'oeil* window and vistas on the wall. This trick visually expands the space by creating the illusion of outside views.
Small windows
If the existing windows are too small, you can pretend you have windows to spare by placing curtains across an entire wall. To lend a greater semblance of reality to the illusion, install some hidden lighting behind the curtains.

To make the most of a room with an insufficient number of windows, give them some help by adding reflective surfaces in the room. Install glass doors or mirrors in wall units, bookcases and cabinets, or room dividers. The light that enters through the window will be increased by reflection off the shiny surfaces.

■

If you have no window, paint one. This trompe l'oeil scene is a fine way of dealing with a window- less room.

■

A stained glass window offers privacy and yet admits a certain amount of light. It's a costly solution, but a highly satisfactory way of dealing with the need for privacy in the bath.

Unsightly views

Where windows look out on unsightly views, the decorative treatment of choice is to minimize or disguise the view while still allowing light to enter. Opaque glass, such as a stained glass or frosted glass, can be employed. Vertical blinds and opaque but translucent (light-admitting) materials such as lace and rice-paper screens block the view yet still admit light.

Glass shelves are another device. Install slender glass shelves in front of the windows and then place potted plants or collectibles such as decorative colored bottles on them. Movable paneled screens also can be used to cover windows.

Courtesy of American Standard

■
Shutters are a good choice for controlling light. If the view isn't especially attractive, they are a highly suitable choice.

WINDOW COVERINGS

Window coverings have both a utilitarian and a decorative function. They help you control the amount of light and air that's admitted to the room and so must provide good filtering of light while not impeding ventilation. A covering can save energy by insulating a room from loss of heat or conditioned cool air. It also can provide some soundproofing by muffling street noise and compensate for deficits such as awkward placement or different-size windows in the same room.

By framing a view, of course, a covering enhances it. Treat a window to an inner curtain of lace or a decorative shade surrounded by curtains and a matching valance. Try pairing laminated shades

■

Blinds don't have to be white. Dark-colored blinds are highly sophisticated.

that match the wallpaper with a coordinating fabric drape and tiebacks, and the window will draw all eyes.

Layered treatments can be costly. If estimates indicate that the desired covering is too expensive, do it one step at a time. Curtain for privacy first, then add decorative layers later on.

As a major contributor to a room's ambience, window coverings are usually best if they are in keeping with the general decorative style. You can choose different treatments for each room. However, give some thought to exterior appearance and, where possible, minimize the distracting effect of different colors and forms at every window. One solution is to use the same color window shades or blinds as a first layer on most of the windows. You can also have curtains lined with the same color lining, which usually is white or off-white.

The two types of treatments can be classified as soft and hard. The major categories of hard coverings are blinds, shades, and shutters. Soft fabric coverings include curtains and such decorative forms of shades as Roman blinds and Austrian or balloon shades. Modern hybrids like soft pleated shades and blinds with fabric slats straddle a line between hard and soft. Multiple treatments often combine both hard and soft coverings at the same window.

Curtains

As you begin to study decorating books and actual rooms, you will see that ways of using fabric at the windows are enormously varied. Besides these resources, the catalog and samples you'll find in many window decor shops and departments will also help you to clarify your ideas on how to treat your own windows.

Just as clothes styles change every few years, so do decorating styles for windows. Recently, for example, so-called Austrian or balloon shades, which are softly shirred fabric coverings that can be pulled up in gathers, have been quite popular. Roman shades or blinds are a more tailored version of a similar construction. By now, the working vocabulary of window styles is enormous. You can choose to reproduce a period window covering or strike out in a new direction.

Still, it's helpful to know the traditional rules: For example, heavy fabrics should always be full length; coverings that go to the sill or all the way down are preferable to three-quarter-length curtains, which almost always have an ungraceful appearance and therefore are used rarely. In order to look luxurious and well tailored, curtains need to be lined. Some owe their beauty to a second interlining that helps them lie flat. The linings are part of the look and therefore necessary, but they add considerably to cost and weight. It's better to select a simpler covering and have it executed beautifully than to choose an elaborate treatment and then skimp on materials or workmanship.

A solid color or a quiet print or textured material is a safer window-covering choice than a flamboyant print. If you do choose the busy fabric, try it out first to make sure it's not too distracting. One way to tone it down is to have a border in a solid color that appears in the print.

Before settling on a window covering, consider the issue of care. All window coverings—even those in the country—ultimately will be harmed by airborne particles of dirt and grit. How difficult will it be to remove, clean, and rehang the curtains? If you have tall windows, be aware that a long length of fabric that is gathered excessively will be quite heavy.

Ready-made headings that can be sewn into the top of the curtain are a boon to home sewers who are making their own. Though top workrooms don't need ready-made headings, the do-it-yourselfer can use them to produce attractive homemade curtains. Headings can be purchased in fabric specialty shops, and with them an adventurous and moderately skilled hand with a sewing machine can make curtains. The type of heading selected has to be the right one for the type of curtain you are sewing.

The amount of material you will need for a curtain depends on the type of heading and the type of

fabric you choose. Here's a guideline. For gathered curtains, figure one and a half times the length of the curtain. For pencil pleats in a medium-weight fabric, figure about twice the length. But if you use sheer netting, you have to allow three times the length because this type of fabric gathers up more finely. Pinch-pleated curtains usually take about twice the length of the curtain for average-weight fabrics and about three times the length for sheers.

■

A low curtain and valance that leaves the top part of the window uncovered admits light while providing privacy.

■

*Wide blinds in rattan
suit this quiet room.*

You can hang curtains so that the rod shows even when the curtain is closed or you can install rods that don't show. A cornice (a boxlike top covering usually of wood) or a valance (a top covering of fabric) can hide the rod entirely whether the curtain is open or closed.

Shades, blinds, and shutters

Consider shades as a first covering for drafty windows. Surveys show that closely woven, tightly fitted, inside-mounted shades with a light-reflecting lining can cut winter heat loss through a window by up to 25 percent and can reduce the summer sun by 55 percent.

Pleated shades are usually all or almost all polyester, because this fabric retains a pleat better than practically any other fiber. Sometimes a small amount of another fiber, such as acrylic or linen, will be added to vary the texture of the shade. Usually custom ordering is required for the more interesting patterns and materials. However, stock pleated shades, usually in white or ivory, are available to fit common window sizes.

If you have an unusual window, such as a skylight, bay window, or window with a rounded top, pleated shades may be the best answer. Treatments for arched windows generally utilize two shades, a stationary, fan-shaped shade to cover the upper arch and a standard operating shade to cover the operative part of the window. A bottom-up pleated shade pulls up instead of down and can screen an unattractive view and provide privacy while still admitting plenty of light.

Blinds can be made of wood, metal, plastic, or fabric. One of their greatest advantages is the ability to screen the interior from view while still admitting a view, air, and light. Blinds offer good control of light for sleeping or watching television.

Though most blinds have horizontal slats, vertical blinds expand the options and are a treatment of choice with sliding doors and windows. When first introduced, vertical blinds were made of hard materials such as metal and PVC. But recently, hundreds

of colors and textures have been made available in fabrics that range from lightweight sheers to heavy tapestry-like light blockers. Though most vertical blinds are still sold on a custom basis, it is possible to buy stock vertical blinds for some popular sizes of patio doors in stores and in mail-order catalogs. All types of blinds can have slats of different colors on each side or can be colored like Joseph's coat, in multiple colors on the same side.

Old-fashioned shutters on the inside of a window are a good choice when you need to keep the glare of the sun out—for example, at a beach house in subtropical or northerly latitudes. Adjustable slats can create the best of two worlds: control of sun entry and an opportunity to see the view by slanting the slats. Hardboard panels with a latticework or sheer fabric insert are other unusual but interesting window treatments. Consider shutters in painted, natural, or stained wood not only for modern interiors but whenever you want a neat and unobtrusive window covering.

■

Vertical blinds are a treatment of choice for sliding glass doors since they can be moved to the side to permit use of the door.

Chapter 6

ACCESSORIES

THE ROOMS MAY be painted, the furniture in place, the bed made and the television set hooked up. But it's not really home until you unpack and set out your possessions. The so-called nonessentials such as art objects, collectibles, photos, books, and memorabilia add the personality that sets your place apart from everybody else's. Without distinctive accessories, you could be like the man who mistakenly enters his neighbor's house one night and can't tell it apart from his own identically arranged abode.

In other eras, when individuality was perhaps not so highly prized as it is in the 1990s, neighboring homes did tend to be similar. Today it's assumed that most people want to live in a setting that reflects their interests. Accessories play an important role in creating that unique environment. Those who crave novelty can provide for it by selecting fairly plain furniture and then using unusual accessories to set the mood. When it's time for a change, swap the accessories for something quite different.

■

Framed family photos personalize a room as no other accessory can.

■ *Use a large number of framed artworks to compete with a strong wall covering.*

Choosing and arranging your objects may seem to be different and not necessarily related activities. But anyone who has purchased a display piece knows that the urge to fill it with whatever looks just right is almost irresistible. If you buy a corner cabinet, you'll almost certainly find yourself eyeing interesting-looking plates to display there.

Often their use dictates where accessories must go. Hardworking pieces, such as clocks, sound equipment, and silver chests need to be put in accessible spots. Lamps must be near a plug, near a chair, and handy to turn on and off. Display and storage pieces may be used as a room's focal point but also have to be kept out of harm's way, which may mean shielding them from direct sunlight and from street view. There is often greater leeway in placing paintings and art objects, but here, too, there is usually an optimum location.

Besides carrying out functional needs and giving people something to look at, accessories, like good soldiers, can be deployed to do whatever needs doing in a room. They can emphasize a focal point. A pair of hurricane lanterns on a fireplace mantel calls attention to the fireplace. They can give a room balance. If all the heavy furniture is on one side of the room and it feels unbalanced, place a commanding accessory such as a grandfather clock or a large potted plant on the other side to correct the imbalance.

If a room is lifeless and dull, you can add brilliantly colored throw cushions, a large bowl filled with a collection of glass balls, an ornate framed mirror, or a display of photos in mirrored frames.

ARRANGING TIPS

Relate the size of an accessory to its background—big pictures on large walls, tall plants on tall walls, delicate pieces on slender shelves. Use an organizing principle when grouping accessories: color, size, texture, shape, or theme.

If you have only small items, group them together to give them mass. For example, instead of setting out two small cactus plants in the middle of a dining table, fill a large, shallow container with pebbles. Buy more plants and put them all on the tray. You could try adding a toy cowboy and horse to create a whimsical setting.

Use color as an organizing tactic. Rather than displaying an unrelated mix of china and glass, raid the cupboard for a selection of blue and white china. For a change, put the blue and white away and substitute a collection of glass candlesticks or wine glasses. Another time, choose ceramics that are all white or black and white pieces. By changing your accessories, you keep a room looking fresh and interesting for the occupants. It's been shown that people cease to see what they are accustomed to seeing, so rearranging is a way of refreshing the eye.

Odd numbers of items look better than even numbers. Choose three or five instead of two or four items to display together. Patterned accessories stand out best when seen against a plain background.

■ *OPPOSITE PAGE:*
These accessories are an indispensable part of this room. They convey a quality of exoticism.

■ *LEFT:*
With accessories, several of the same thing (in this case, candlestands) add up to more than the sum of the parts.

A decorator created a unique wall hanging from a large piece of Burmese embroidered fabric by having it stuffed to give it dimension and bring out its interesting and unique pattern. She then mounted it on silk linen and framed it in gold leaf before hanging it on a wall.

Another chose three colorful 22-inch (55-cm) Chinese porcelain jardinieres. She had a rosewood base made for each one and placed them at equidistance on the floor of a dining room. A one-inch- (2.5-cm-) thick glass top placed on top did not obscure the jardinieres but did make a decorative dining table.

Antiquities such as etched bronze drums from Thailand, old Korean containers, and wedding baskets from Indonesia can become cocktail table bases. Korean coin chests in wood with iron hardware become side tables with the added bonus of storage capacity.

FURNITURE FOR COLLECTIONS

A curio cabinet is an extremely flexible display case for collectibles. Ideal locations for the cabinets include entryways, hallways, and unused wall areas or in a wall—spaces that may be going to waste at present. Cabinets also work well bunched to make a display wall in a living room, dining room, or den.

Besides taking into account the style of the room and other furnishings, consider what will be displayed inside the curio when selecting it. A massive cabinet would dwarf a display of small, delicate items, even a large number of them. Instead of showing an entire collection of diminutive objects in a large curio, it would be more appealing to choose a small cabinet to show off a few special items and to rotate the display so that there is always something new to look at and enjoy.

Originally, curios were small cabinets for the storage and display of small "curiosities." They were typically only about a foot (30 cm) or so wide, a foot deep and 64 inches (162 cm) high. Today they come in a great assortment of sizes from slender cabinets to china size, and bunching cabinets can be stacked to form walls of display space. Features include

■
Using the same frame for several prints hung together is a unifying device.

Unexpected accessories

One of the marks of an interesting room is the unexpected touches it contains, especially in the form of accessories. These do not have to be costly. Relatively affordable ethnic accessories from the Far East can become a focal point in a room. Indian paintings on fabric known as *pichwais* and Burmese embroideries are selected by those seeking distinction without breaking the bank.

The most creative individuals rarely use an item exactly as found. They further embellish it to make it more arresting and unusual. Here are some actual examples.

interior lighting, which can be controlled on a dimmer, a leveling guide, mirrored backs, plate rails, and security locks. Angled cabinets provide as many as five or six sides of glass for in-the-round viewing.

If the cabinet has a wood center shelf (required for structural strength in larger sizes), there has to be a source of light in the bottom of the cabinet. Often it is a fluorescent light. But the more expensive models may have incandescent light in the bottom, which is considered preferable because it is softer and more flattering to objects.

Better cabinets can usually be leveled from the inside bottom with a screwdriver. They offer a potential adjustment of from 2 to 2.5 inches (5 to 6.3 cm). Bunching several cabinets can be a tricky installation.

Although the curio selected should relate comfortably to the other furniture in the room, the cabinetry itself is not the primary style issue. The most successful curios are almost unobtrusive in style, since their purpose is to show off the pieces that are displayed. Because they are usually mostly glass and often have either a glass or mirrored back, they are not bulky in appearance.

Choose open shelves on which to display objects based on the objects themselves. Heavy pieces need durable shelves that can bear their weight safely. Make sure that shelves are mounted correctly. The size and number of shelves should be keyed to the size of wall on which they are located. Don't use up every last inch (cm) of space. Allow enough space so that the shelf does not appear crowded.

ACCESSORIES DON'T HAVE TO COST A LOT

You can use accessories to achieve a feeling of richness in a room that may be characterless even if you have a tiny budget. A few expensive needlepoint pillows, a small item of antique furniture, a collection of porcelain or crystal, or a paisley shawl made from a yard (1 m) of fabric and some trimming give a room a rich feeling, thus contributing far more than their cost to the overall effect of a room.

Within the boundaries of the general theme, rooms are more interesting when they hold a few surprises. In a restrained room, a single ornate antique or reproduction provides a welcome contrast. A handmade or antique accessory such as a rug or a lacquered box lends distinction.

Original yet inexpensive collectibles are tapestry fragments, old baskets, pictorial ceramic tiles, perfume bottles, and unmatched pieces of china. Concentrate on only one form, such as dinner plates or cups and saucers. You can make bits of tapestry go farther on throw cushions by backing them with brocade or velvet. If the fragments are large enough, you can hang them on the wall or at the windows. Nail baskets to the wall facing out or group them on a shelf. Plates lend distinction to an empty wall when hung in a circular, vertical, or horizontal arrangement.

■ *ABOVE:*
If you want to emphasize the horizontal dimension, select an accessory that draws the eye across the wall.

■ *RIGHT:*
A vitrine not only organizes a collection of valuable antiquities, it also keeps it safe.

■ *A Welsh dresser is used to display a collection of ceramics. It is also an important focal point in this room.*

■ *OPPOSITE PAGE: Some collectibles, such as these antique Portuguese and Dutch tiles, can be attractively displayed in kitchen or bathroom for an equally charming effect.*

Many appealing and character-rich accessories started life as something else. They include outmoded old porcelain basins, brass spittoons, and odd pieces of china. Today we have little use for spittoons that in the eighteenth and nineteenth centuries were customary appurtenances in fashionable interiors. But we do need larger containers suitable for a party; as planters and ashtrays, these containers function very well.

Other recycled containers include shells that can be used as ashtrays, soap dishes, or food servers. Large conch shells make excellent centerpieces on a dining table when filled with flowers and baby vegetables.

An old-fashioned cabinet that once held clothing or food is more likely to hold stereo equipment and a television set today. Ornate wrought-iron bases from old sewing machines are often turned into table bases. You can convert circular and half-moon windows (find them in architectural-antique outlets) into unusual mirrors by having the frame refinished and replacing the glass with mirrors.

For a modest expenditure, you can make coffee tables out of lobster traps and a sheet of glass and throw loose fabric over threadbare sofas and chairs.

Turn tin cans into candle holders by punching holes in them in a decorative pattern, and turn building parts into brackets to hold a shelf.

Tables can be made out of old wooden shipping crates with interesting stenciled lettering, sections of a tree trunk, old doors and cans glued together in a large cube and surmounted by a clear acrylic top.

Make a lighted bedside table out of two chrome wheel rims, a piece of glass 13 inches (33 cm) in diameter, and a light bulb and socket. The execution is simplicity itself. The rims are heavy enough to stand securely without any adhesive.

Reuse dome-shaped silver vegetable dish covers as planters by having the covers cut in half and a new flat back soldered on to each half to create two half-moon planters, which can be filled with ivy and hung on the dining-room wall.

Since a bowling pin is already roughly the shape of a torso and head, old bowling pins can be turned into decorative hatstands or head sculptures with the addition of headgear and fabric.

HANGING ARTWORK AND WALL DECOR

You won't go wrong if you follow the general rules of composition when hanging art on the walls. If pictures are hung hit or miss, it's distracting. Adopt an inverted V-shape configuration to provide unity and organization. For example, set two lamps at either side of a sofa and center a large picture over the sofa.

In a small room with low ceilings, it's a mistake to hang several very large pictures close together. In a large room, it's hard to make a group of insignificant pictures look good unless you reinforce their impact in frames and site selection.

When pictures are hung over or near furniture, try to create a feeling of harmony between the two by relating the frames and subject matter to the furniture—perhaps by aligning them in a symmetrical arrangement or matching the woods or choosing matting that matches the upholstery color.

■

Flowers against a lattice-work background lend a year-round feeling of springtime.

© Jennifer Levy

■

Hang a quilt on the wall if you want to make a strong graphic impression. In this room, the throw pillows echo the quilt and strengthen the overall effect.

© Jennifer Levy

At times, it will be more practical to hang a picture higher on the wall—for example, above a table. Hanging pictures too high, however, leaves a gap space that disturbs a room's balance. So fill the space below the picture with a decorative object, such as a vase of flowers. The vase becomes a link that ties the table to the picture in a unified visual composition. Generally speaking, hang art at eye level, basing your decision about what constitutes eye level on whether viewers will be mainly standing or sitting.

Certain areas in the home traditionally serve as sites for large works of art. One expects to see a large picture above a sofa, over a fireplace, or in a foyer above a console table. In each instance a mix of pictures hung as a group can substitute for the single large picture.

When you want to lend importance to a work of art, use a mat, or mount, to set it off. The mat also makes the work more visible by creating space around it. Deciding on mat size is usually a matter of eyeing the mat and picture together. A rule of thumb is to choose a mat a bit deeper on the bottom to add a feeling of substance and weight.

In frame selection, one ploy is to choose a frame to harmonize with the subject matter of the picture—a wood frame around a painting of trees, bleached wood for a beach scene, a mat color that echoes a color in the work itself, a black frame on a black-and-white etching.

The first priority is to match the picture to the frame rather than the frame to the room. If a work is striking, choose a dramatic frame. If the piece is delicate, don't upstage or overwhelm it with too powerful a frame. A skimpy, too-narrow frame makes the picture seem fragile and cramped. A surround that is too large, however, creates the impression that the work inside it is insignificant.

There are several options when choosing framing materials. The more expensive is known as museum or conservation framing and employs acid-free cotton rag paper for mats and backing. The artwork is attached with acid-free tape or glue. A museum type of framing job usually separates artwork from the glass so they do not touch. Sometimes, the glass is ultraviolet-resistant, which is a good idea if exposure to excessive sunlight is expected to occur. Too much sun can fade pigments right through ordinary glass. Glare-free glass is also available, although at about twice the cost of ordinary picture glass. The less expensive method of framing calls for wood-pulp paper, which is half the price of rag paper. Labor costs are about the same.

When you need to fill a large expanse of wall without having an "important" painting for it, try grouping several pictures in a large-scale arrangement. Experiment on the floor before hanging the works on the wall by measuring the wall space and marking an area of the floor that is the same size. Rearrange the items until you find an overall shape that is pleasing and provides the needed sense of order.

In a wall display, it's often more interesting to mix paintings, prints, posters, and watercolors with photographs, maps, swatches of lace or tapestry fragments, china plates, even shadow boxes in which objects such as antique spoons or dried flowers are displayed. Flat things such as old swords can be hung on a mixed wall of art without any framing at all.

Personal memorabilia can be included in a wall arrangement. Some possibilities: the lyrics of your favorite song, the menu from a special dinner, a recipe, a favorite poem, famous autograph, child's artwork, an award, a cartoon, family photos, even a scorecard with your best golf game.

Not too many years ago it was considered most appropriate to hang pictures against a white wall. Today, we happily accept a picture against patterned wallpaper or a decorated and colored wall surface. But when hanging artworks against wallpaper, especially strongly patterned wallpaper, remember that busy backgrounds need strong pictures and frames. You can avoid a jarring note by choosing pictures that complement the decorative period of the room or introducing a color in the wallpaper in the mat or frame surrounding the artwork. Avoid selecting a frame that is particularly

decorative for a wall with heavily patterned wallpaper. The same frame is likely to look much better against textured paper or fabric in a solid color. Dark walls are good backdrops for monochrome works like pen-and-ink drawings or strong linear architectural prints.

A new style in decorating today is to surround oneself with framed family photos. The memorabilia are displayed on a table or mantel in a mix of old and new frames in a variety of materials. Often, small knickknacks are mixed in a way that is particularly appealing in country style rooms. Other places to hang photos and small works include hallways and staircases.

■ *OPPOSITE PAGE:*
When appropriately used, posters and enlarged photographs are every bit as decorative as framed paintings, and far less expensive.

■ *BELOW:*
African sculptures are so powerful as art objects that they can almost stand alone.

U*Part Three*
UPDATING YOUR HOME
FOR THE NINETIES

Introduction

IN THIS SECTION, we will apply the principles acquired so far to creating specific rooms that will give pleasure today, tomorrow, and into the new century. As a general principle, the greatest difference between past and present is that prescribed activities and furnishings for specific rooms have largely disappeared.

The new way of thinking sees the home as an organic whole, rather than a constellation of rooms. It is still true that the foyer, living room, and dining area function as places of public gathering, that bedrooms are sheltered from view, and that special attention is given to functional utility in work spaces such as the kitchen and laundry. However, a more informal style of living, a busier lifestyle, and a wider range of activities at home contribute to a freer use of space.

The most successful rooms today are attractive enough to welcome visitors and comfortable enough to support private leisure activities. If you live in a loft, it's unlikely that you have a separate foyer, living room, dining room, and kitchen. You may have chosen the space specifically because you wanted to break out of a traditional environment. Yet you have to plan for the functions carried out in such rooms, even if you don't have them. You will still enter laden with packages, hang up coats, welcome guests, invite them to sit down, serve meals, and so on.

We do not all pursue the same lifestyle. Not everyone dines at 7, often with guests, and retires at 11. But we all engage in greeting, entertaining, relaxing, dining, cooking, cleaning, storing possessions and retrieving them, and resting.

As part of the process of decorating and furnishing a residence, consider where you will do the things you like to do and make sure you have the necessary furnishings. A comfortable residence is one that supports you in your daily activities, regardless of where you carry them out.

■ *Both of these rooms are informal, but it's clear that different people occupy each one. The room on the opposite page is a low-key space in which the view of the outdoors plays an important part. The room on the left is a dramatic space that can hold its own against the outdoors because of the brilliance of the color and the extensive use of pattern.*

Chapter 1

Rooms for Greeting, Entertaining, and Relaxing

A foyer as impressive as this one deserves special treatment; after all, the foyer welcomes visitors to your home. The gold trim gives this room a particularly regal appearance.

THE ENTRYWAY

A foyer or entryway should be a welcoming space that simplifies the logistics of entering, exiting, greeting visitors, and receiving packages and mail. To do all these tasks well, it takes practical surfaces, functional furniture, and decoration in harmony with the rooms to which it leads.

No foyer is complete without a surface on which to set down packages, mail, a purse, or a hat. A logical addition is a mirror since many people like to check their appearance just before going in or out. If there is room for it, a place to sit down is useful. Space given over to display an object of beauty such as a vase of flowers amply repays the small area it occupies.

An entryway is such a useful appurtenance that it is worth adding if it doesn't exist. Making an entryway with a paneled screen is one of the least expensive and most flexible ways to create a separate foyer. At the other extreme, you could build a small vestibule onto the front of the house. The new space will conserve heat as well as provide a place to greet people. Often a full or half wall can be constructed to screen off the area near the door. This can be a constructed surface or one made by placing a piece of furniture finished on both sides between the door and the rest of the room. Faux or real architectural columns offer partial screening. Tall bookcases not only create a movable wall; they also can be used to store books, magazines, and papers.

If you find it difficult to visualize how a freestanding wall or a large piece of furniture will affect the layout of the entire room, try out your idea by making a cardboard dummy in the projected size and shape. Paper carton material is usually available free from the supermarket, and for the relatively small trouble and expense, the dummy piece can reduce the risk of adding something permanent and expensive that you don't like.

Often, the space allotted to the foyer is confining. Relieve the claustrophobic feeling by mirroring one wall or hanging a mirror on it. Lighting can visually expand the space. Use recessed spotlights, track lighting, wall-mounted sconces, a ceiling fixture or a combination of these. If there's no natural light, install concealed cove lighting where the ceiling and wall meet to create the illusion of natural light. Another way to further this illusion is to turn a small niche into a lighted alcove in which you place a narrow piece of furniture or a decorative statue on a pedestal. Light the alcove from below or above.

Regardless of the colors and design theme you choose, for practicality, select a hard-wearing floor that can withstand tracked-in mud, snow, and rain. A traditional foyer floor that has withstood the test of time is a pattern of square black and white marble, ceramic, or vinyl tiles laid diagonally to visually expand the space. A low-cost improvement

■

Provide a table on which parcels and mail can be collected in the entry.

■

If you are lucky enough to have a graceful stairway, it can serve as a focal point for the entry area.

for a discolored wood floor is to paint or stencil a pattern and protect it with a layer of polyurethane. A small rug that can be washed or cleaned can turn any type of floor into one that is attractive and easy to maintain.

Decorating a foyer

Since an entryway is a space that is passed through rather than inhabited, you can afford to be more extravagant and daring when decorating than you could be in a room. Above all else, a foyer can be a space for drama and excitement, a place to use exuberant color or a highly patterned wallcovering. Its diminutive size means it takes only a bit of a costly and exotic decorative material to make an impact. So you can splurge on marble, imported tile, designer wallpaper, or a specialty paint job.

Foyers should be in character with the rest of the house. If, for example, you are emphasizing a country theme, choose elements such as a mural in naive style or wallpaper or painted borders in a suitable design. At less expense, buy an art poster and hang it or display a rough stoneware jug or copper basin with dried flowers.

It is typical in traditional homes for the foyer to be situated between the living room and dining room. In that case, tie the two rooms together by emphasizing a color in the foyer that is present in both rooms. If the living room is mostly beige, add red accents in pillows, window treatment, upholstery fabric, or floor covering. In the dining room choose a fabric or wall covering with red in it. Then create a red foyer. The dramatic design will unite all three rooms. You may not be able to live with a red living room, but a red foyer is invigorating.

Some homes, such as early-twentieth-century cottages, are meant to open directly onto the living room. In that case, don't try to disguise the absence of a foyer. Instead, hunt for an antique that can function as an aid to reception all by itself; one example is that common nineteenth-century item known as a hall tree. It combines a bench, mirror, and hooks in a single piece.

Frequently, modern apartment layouts have a windowless space that is just large enough to accommodate a dining table and four chairs and is designated on the builder's floor plan as a dining area. "Forget it," says the American designer Beverly Ellsley. "Most people would prefer not to eat a meal in a tiny, windowless room. Instead, use the space as a foyer and find another place for a dining table," she advises.

THE LIVING ROOM

It follows from the name alone that your living room should be geared to the way you live. You'll know how to begin the process of furnishing and decorating once you have summarized the kinds of activities you will pursue in the room. Of course, these vary, but for most people the main items on the list

▪

This comfortable room is clearly designed for entertaining company: there are plenty of chairs and a lot of space; a grand piano fills one wall; and a dry bar nestles in the back.

are relaxing at home (perhaps watching television, listening to music, reading, or playing games at a table) and entertaining informally and on a grander scale. A living room should work equally well for day- and nighttime activities. Lighting and window treatments are important here. Look at colors, textures, and fabrics under artificial light as well as daylight before you select them.

The living room's style and the decorative objects on display are a visual and functional "statement" about your interests and aspirations. This is where the choice of accessories and artworks (see Chapter 6 in Part Two) and the selection of a decorative theme (Part Four) come in.

In most households where people of different ages and interests share the living room, zoning the space to accommodate several different activities at the same time is an excellent idea. Use furniture placement, area rugs, accessories, and lighting to help you create these zones of activity. It helps if the room is of generous proportions, which is ideal for a living room.

One way to break up the space in a large, symmetrical living room is to establish a strong focal point in the center of the room. You might start with a large round table on which there's a floral arrangement or sculpture and over which there's a hanging fixture such as a chandelier. This strong center effectively divides the room into two—or if wide enough, four—separate areas. Maintain continuity with color scheme, materials, and general stylistic themes. A 20-by-40-foot (6.1-by-12.2-m) living room most likely could accommodate a dining and game table and chairs, a conversation area, and a place to watch television and listen to music.

Changes in level and angle also effectively zone a large room. People enjoy a large space more if they have something interesting to look at. Overscaled accessories and large works of art, such as a six-panel Oriental screen or a framed advertising poster, can break up long expanses of wall. A pair of columns is effective in visually dividing a wall, as are niches that can be created with columns or furniture placement. Fill a niche with bookshelves

or with a pedestal on which you display an artwork or vase of flowers. Other good space dividers in a big room are display cabinets and oversize plants.

Decorating around a piano

A piano can be a wonderful addition to a living room in a household where music is valued. Grand pianos come in small, medium, and large sizes, taking from 5 to 9 feet (1.6 to 3 m) of depth in a room. An upright comes in heights that range from 36 inches (92 cm) for a spinet to 44 inches (112 cm) for the largest studio size.

There are two basic approaches to decorating with a piano: Flaunt it or integrate it. The grand piano with its dramatic curve is best suited to the first approach. Treat it like sculpture and position it so that its curved shape juts into the room.

One of the most dramatic treatments is to set the instrument on a raised platform and make it a focal point in the room. If a platform isn't practical or desirable, you can achieve the same effect by lowering the ceiling directly over the piano. Light can be used to highlight a piano without any structural changes at all. Directional lights of a soft pink character give it a misty romantic aura. A harder more diamondlike light, such as the light from a halogen source, imparts a different quality. Put lights on a dimmer so you can turn these special effects on and off.

As long as you have the piano, consider arranging it for musical soirées so that chairs can be pulled up to create a listening area.

An upright piano is less intrusive than a grand. You could place it against an otherwise empty short wall or you could make it a part of the home-entertainment wall and install cabinetry around it to hold stereo components, cassettes, and tapes. Carrying the idea of integration to its most extreme lengths, you could recess an upright into a wall and surround it with built-ins so that only the keyboard protrudes.

The piano is a delicate instrument with specific physical needs. Guard especially against exposure

■

For many people, listening to music is one of the most important activities in the living room. This room is organized around a wall of entertainment components.

to abrupt changes in temperature, which damage the mechanism. Don't put it next to frequently opened outside doors or in front of a picture window, heating duct, or radiator. The ideal temperature is a constant 72°F (22°C); humidity of 40 percent is considered perfect.

The living room as media center

The living room often includes a television set, videocassette player, and stereo equipment. These, along with storage space for cassettes and disks, are the basics of a home-entertainment center. Decorating decisions make a difference in your enjoyment of the room as a listening and viewing environment. You can improve the room's acoustics by choosing the right fabrics and placing the speakers well.

For good sound reproduction, it's important to break up the boxiness of the typical square room by providing a variety of surfaces off which the sound waves can bounce. Soft surfaces absorb sound, while hard surfaces cause it to reverberate into the room, so a combination of soft and hard surfaces at various angles creates the richest sound.

The ceiling and floor are the most obvious places to provide a contrast. By carpeting the floor and leaving the ceiling bare, you have made a good acoustical decorating decision. Soft materials need cover only a portion of a surface, so a rug and draperies can also provide the needed softness if you prefer bare wood floors. Textured wall coverings, even artworks, can also absorb sound.

If you are thinking of a giant television screen, you need a room large enough to accommodate it. To minimize the decorative distraction of a large, blank, 6-foot (2-m) screen, mount it in a bookcase wall behind shutters, blinds, or curtains.

If your sound system includes two separate loudspeakers, as most do, the sound you hear will be very much affected by the placement of those speakers. Rooms are too varied for any exact rules on where to place speakers, but general guidelines can provide a beginning. After that, it is a matter of subjecting the arrangement to a listening test.

■
*Use the living room walls
for storage; provide com-
fortable seating, table
and chairs for games or
impromptu meals, and
you will have the makings
of a living room in keep-
ing with today's way of
life.*

For the best sound, listeners should be roughly the same distance from the left and right speakers. The size and shape of the speakers are a clue to where the manufacturer thinks they will sound best. Small bookcase speakers are meant to sit in or on a bookcase and usually sound better if placed above the eye level of seated listeners. The larger vertical speakers are meant to rest directly on the floor or in the bottom part of a wall system or bookcase. Speakers with unfinished backs are supposed to go against the wall. Those with a finished back are usually designed to be placed a few feet (60 cm) out from the wall.

A small rug on the floor a few feet in front of the speakers can work wonders on sound quality. Other surfaces near speakers can be softened with wall hangings, by closing the curtains, or by filling the bookshelves with books. Glass is a very harsh sound reflector. If you can see your speakers in a mirror, move the mirror or the speaker.

Today's popular diagonal room arrangements can contribute to good listening since a bulky mass set on the diagonal breaks up the parallel surfaces of a boxy room. A three-panel screen is another decorating device that can improve the sound in your room. A screen placed on the diagonal in one corner of the room provides a new surface for the sound to bounce off.

Home-entertainment centers tend to be places where people sprawl and eat crumbly snack food, so it will be more satisfactory if furnished for comfort and durability. Choose sturdy seating that can take a certain amount of abuse and fabrics that disguise dirt and stains and are easy to clean. Wood-framed, loose-cushion sofas and settees, and vinyl or leather easy chairs with matching ottomans or recliners come to mind as good seating selections. Sectionals and modulars that can be reconfigured for unobstructed views of the big screen are also a good idea.

On one hand, highly textured materials such as tweed and linens are better for acoustics than smooth and slick materials such as leather and silk. On the other hand, a totally soft textured room in which fabric is used with abandon is not the best listening environment because it leads to a deadening condition in which all the sound is swallowed up by the furnishings.

For a neater room, make sure to plan for storage furniture with at least one or two enclosed spaces to accommodate all those disks and cassettes and video games if you have them. Cabinetry should have adequate ventilation at the rear and there should be access to the back of the components for inevitable repairs.

The test of a good media room is how the music and speech sound. Incidentally, following these guidelines also enhances the sounds of conversation and live music.

New ideas in home electronics

Within the next decade or so, electronics will make what the home building industry calls the smart home a realistic option. Such homes will be equipped with integrated controls for security, communications, and home entertainment.

Already taking advantage of new electronics products, some people are beginning to plan in advance for delivery of music and radio and television programs throughout the house. Systems designed so components in one room can be turned on and off in another room via remote control allow sound sources to be played through loudspeakers in different rooms at the same time. The end result is that a single set of components can make music available in every room at the touch of a button.

By the end of the 1990s, a predicted 30 to 40 percent of new homes will have a central audio-video system, although heretofore multiroom systems have been available mainly as a custom option through specialty audio installers.

With a multiroom system, you could install one high-quality music system in the living room and have access to it from remote speakers mounted in each room. A wall-mounted keypad control in each room with a set of speakers could turn such components as a cassette and CD player, turntable, and radio on and off. The controls also make it possible to switch from one source to another—say, radio to CD player—and to change the radio station.

■ *High-tech stereo equipment comes in a wide variety of shapes and sizes; choose a system that produces enough sound to fill the listening room.*

The only disadvantage of a multiroom system is that you have to load what you want to hear into the main system, which may be in another room. That little problem is already being dealt with through the development of automatic changers for all audio and video sources. The technology of CD changers is furthest along. A ten-disk changer is common and a one-hundred-disk changer is a well-known custom installation. Audiocassette changers that accommodate six cassettes at a time are available, and a company in San Francisco is developing a changer that will store and play twenty-eight videos at a time.

Upgrading a living room

A survey of members of the American Society of Interior Designers disclosed that the most common residential decorating project undertaken by designers was redoing a living room. There is reason to believe that the living room is also the do-it-yourself project, too. Most people regard a well-furnished living room as the centerpiece of a lovely home.

If you are dissatisfied with your living room, ask yourself what exactly is bothering you. Perhaps it's an awkward floor plan. The room may have become a thoroughfare for everyone in the family and therefore a catchall for accumulated possessions. There may be no peaceful and orderly place to sit down and read or to have a conversation.

Maybe specific items of furniture or accessories are unattractive, the wrong color, or simply missing. There may not be enough bookcases or table lamps or easy chairs. Perhaps there's no table large enough to accommodate your Wednesday-night bridge group. It could be that you no longer like the style of the room. Or the room's surfaces may be what need attention—a new rug, a paint job or wallpaper, more compelling window treatments.

Once you've analyzed the problem, you can decide how to proceed. If—as is so often the situation—you'd like to upgrade the living room quickly without spending a great deal of money, consider these suggestions:

© Phillip Ennis

A formal space is one that is arranged symmetrically, as in the all-white living room. Notice that the two arrangements of plants are lit from below. At night, these lights will throw interesting shadows on the ceiling.

New lighting

Buy a canister light to hide behind a table, chest or large planter. It has a powerful impact in a room at night if placed so that interesting shadows are cast on the ceiling and wall. Put the light on a timer so it is on when you arrive home after dark.

Partial paint job

Paint two walls and the ceiling of the room in a strong color. Place your largest piece of furniture (which in most cases may be the sofa or a cabinet) against one of the newly painted walls to create a focal point.

Hide a flaw

Disguise a feature if you can't abide it, yet can't replace it. Maybe it's olive green, wall-to-wall carpeting or wallpaper that clashes with the rest of the room. While awaiting the time and money to change the eyesore, camouflage it.

Cover the offending carpet with small rugs in every size. Orientals and area rugs of any design are fine together. Put the largest rug in front of the sofa. Work from the largest out to the rest of the carpeted floor. Keep at least 10 inches (25 cm) of space between the different rugs.

© Jennifer Levy

■

This chair and console—two important Chinese pieces—would create distinction in any room.

Cover dreary or garish walls with collections—pictures of every size and all types of frames. You can frame photos, memorabilia, children's paintings, interesting fabric scraps. You can hang plates, antique advertising signs, architectural elements. Begin your wall arrangements about 6 inches (15 cm) from the ceiling with the largest item in the center of the group, moving out and down as you go. This ploy not only hides a wall you hate; it also dramatizes a small room and warms up a large one.

Rearrange the furniture

If rooms seem uninteresting, gain a fresh perspective by moving furniture and accessories around. Bedroom chests, mirrors, and bedside tables can go into the foyer or living room. You can also give your furniture a new look by camouflaging it with fabric. Cover a round table with fabric to the floor. If you need more storage space for bulky items, a skirted table provides a good hiding place for boxes or extra pillows or blankets, which can be stashed under the table out of sight.

Often what's wrong is a subtle lack of harmony between major items of furniture. A modern wall system that's stark and lacking in ornamentation stands out unpleasantly in a generally traditional room.

You can decoratively integrate a wall system or modular units into a traditional room with the artful application of molding, extending it along the rest of the wall at ceiling or baseboard height. If that's not feasible, make the units less obtrusive by painting them the same color as the walls. If you don't want to touch the cabinet, finish the wall to match the storage units. Painting a portion of the front molding of the storage pieces is another option. A charming touch in a country room is to line the back of open bookshelves with a fabric or wallpaper that is used elsewhere in the room.

Buy one great object

If your budget allows for one new item, consider something from this list: a three-panel screen, low chest or pair of chests, rocking chair, decorative clock, upholstered dining chairs that can also double as guest seating in the living room, game table, modular storage components that can be added to or rearranged.

Be crafty

Make a habit of collecting lengths of fabric, which can be used for bedspreads, table covers, pillow-square coverings, and decorating walls that are unappealing in color or pattern.

Turn ordinary silk lampshades into custom wonders with store-bought dye and purchased commercial trims applied with glue. Dye a new, plain white

©image/dennis krukowski. Design: J. Allen Murphy/Eclectic Inc

■

A large group of paper-weights arranged on a lamp table are a charming accent in a living room. You can use collections such as this to add excitement to almost any room.

lampshade pale pink and apply a fringe trim in pink and green at the base and a braid trim with the same colors at the top.

Mix good pieces with secondhand buys to improve the look of the finds. Paint secondhand furniture and then pair it with a good rug, chair, cabinet, or painting. Choose a distinctive fabric and re-cover old sofas for less than it costs to replace them. A floor or table easel gives instant importance to a picture, even if it is only a framed poster.

Start a collection

Use collectibles to give your home personal distinction. Original yet inexpensive collectibles are tapestry fragments, old baskets, pictorial ceramic tiles, perfume bottles, unmatched pieces of china, and dinner plates or cups and saucers. You can make throw pillows of bits of tapestry by backing with brocade or velvet. If the fragments are large enough, you can hang them on the wall or at the windows.

The formal dining room remains one of the most desired rooms, despite reports of its demise.

THE DINING ROOM

Reports of the demise of the formal dining room have turned out to be greatly exaggerated. A recent survey of decorating preferences found that a majority of those queried said they personally would gladly give up an extra bedroom in order to have a dining room.

Regardless of whether it's situated in its own space or in part of another room, a dining area should be a place apart with ample room for a table large enough to accommodate those who regularly eat together. So long as the places can be set, the meal eaten, and the table cleared with a minimum of interference from other activities, the table doesn't have to occupy a separate room. A location in a large kitchen or a shared dining-living area works perfectly well.

A dining table with leaves can add flexibility if you'd like the option of seating a larger crowd for special occasions. Chairs should provide good back support and be selected in relation to the height of the table. Adequate lighting and ventilation are also essential for comfort.

Since convenience will be greatly enhanced if dishes and serving ware can be stored near their place of use, storage furniture such as a sideboard and a china cabinet should be considered if there's room for them.

Buffet meals are a fine method of entertaining in households without outside help, so a buffet server is desirable. A portable server on casters with a durable top and a tea trolley are examples of flexible furniture that many people find useful. These pieces come in many different styles and materials.

■

This modern dining area is defined through the use of extra space around the table, the lighting fixture above the table, and the powerful artwork that fills the wall behind it.

Formerly, dining room suites in which all the furniture matched were the norm. A more adventurous spirit is abroad in the land. Mixing antique chairs with a contemporary table, or vice versa, is common. The serving pieces may easily be in one design theme while the table and chairs are in another. Contemporary art in a traditional room or antique paintings with a glass table and metal-framed modern chairs are fine. Open shelves or a lighted glass-front china cabinet: It's entirely a question of what looks good and works for you.

Besides the more formal dining table and chairs, an informal spot for pickup meals and snacks is a great convenience. As a rule, this second spot is best located in or adjacent to the kitchen. If your lifestyle is informal, space is limited, or you have an open-plan kitchen and dining room, there's no sin-

gle good reason the same table and chairs can't serve both for all meals.

The most common arrangement of dining table and chairs is in the center of the room or dining area. This central placement of round, square, or rectangular table permits easy access and efficient service, especially if a serving person will occasionally be employed. Placing a rectangular table with one of the short ends against the wall takes less floor area and can be a good device for making the best of a small dining room. If the dining table will do double duty as a desk or work surface, this setup also has advantages. Another plan places the table in the corner with a built-in bench or banquette for some of the seating. Though the banquette is somewhat inaccessible, this arrangement works well if space is very limited.

If you are combining a dining room with a living room or family room, make sure the furniture that you plan to integrate is compatible. To avoid that cluttered, uncomfortable look, separate the conversational area and dining area. You can visually reinforce the separation with a piece of furniture, such as a buffet or cabinet that accentuates it. A folding screen or a half wall made by lining up bookcases are other devices that accomplish the same effect. If the furniture is a little taller than table height, it screens off the unattractive aftermath of a meal. Separating living and dining areas enables you to maintain a desirable separation when entertaining between hors d'oeuvres and the meal itself.

A long sofa with its back to the dining area is a good room divider. Dramatic lighting with dimmers can visually separate areas.

Secondary dining room activities

In periods when an informal style of living is dominant, as in the recent past, the appeal of a separate dining room is called into question. So the idea of a room devoted solely to dining began to seem outmoded during the past few decades.

It is a good idea for the dining room to be suited to easily accomodate other household activities. It can be, for example, the place where paperwork and homework are done, where hobbies such as sewing or crafts are pursued, where a decorative collection is displayed, where card games and board games are played, where the children gather to color, where meetings of community groups to which a household member belongs are held. It can even serve as a quiet place to sit down in the morning and have a cup of coffee and read the newspaper.

If any or all of these activities will be taking place, plan for them as best you can. A separate desk set up in a corner or near a window, with a telephone handy, can free the big table for other uses. Shelves can be mounted along one wall to display a collection that then becomes a principal decorative aspect of the room. Choose furniture that will enhance whatever activities you plan. Perhaps chairs

Design: Janice Gewirtz, Photo: David Anderson

■ *ABOVE:*

Who says a dining room has to be kept solely for meals? This room can be converted to a working space. The area near the window is an excellent spot for serious deskwork. Move the chairs away from the window and you have a buffet surface.

■ *OPPOSITE PAGE:*

It's helpful to have a storage piece near the dining table, where you can keep the tableware that is generally used for formal dining.

on casters will make it easier to hold meetings or to rearrange the room. A subdued color scheme or tailored wall coverings may be best. Then when it is time for a party, flowers, balloons, candles, and table decor can provide the festive note.

Being able to welcome family, friends, and acquaintances is so much a part of the reason for expending extra effort to decorate a home. So it is appropriate to consider the ways in which decorating decisions can contribute to the ease of entertaining. Decorators, incidentally, often report that many of their clients telephone for advice when planning a celebration such as a child's engagement or a festive holiday party—an interesting confirmation of the fact that there is a strong relationship between decorating and entertaining. Plan enough storage space and flexible furniture to accommodate party gear and groups and you are likely to feel more comfortable about giving parties.

Entertaining pointers

■ Set up a party closet in which you store linens, interesting centerpieces, and unusual serving dishes. Permanent arrangements of dried or silk flowers can be stored for many years.

■ Create an element of surprise on your dining table. Often this can be done with whimsical centerpieces or decorations, such as statues or miniatures.

■ If you have a large house with several dining areas, set a party table ahead of time so there's time to create special effects. Keep a stock of centerpieces and dried flower arrangements.

■ Mix different patterns of utensils and dishes. Use one pattern for each course or mix and match in the same course.

■ Plan menus to minimize preparation time. Desserts and main dishes often can be made in advance. Vegetables usually taste best when freshly prepared. Make a few large dishes rather than many small ones.

■ Key ethnic foods to the table decorations. For example, serve a Chinese meal on a table set with Asian china and provide chopsticks as well as regular utensils.

■ Give easy parties such as a dessert party at which guests help themselves to five or six flavors of homemade ice cream and their choice of toppings.

■ Gear the table to the people who will be entertained. If holidays are focused around family and children, don't set a table with priceless glasses and china.

■ Key placemats or a tablecloth and napkins to the particular holiday—blue for Hanukkah, pastels for Easter, red and green with touches of glitter for Christmas.

This spectacular room, with glass ceiling and chandelier, is an example of an outdoor room in which the occupants are protected from the elements while enjoying them.

THE OUTDOOR ROOM

The outdoor area around the house can serve as a warm-weather extension of interior living spaces. Though an outdoor "room" often has no roof or walls, it can be a place for cooking, dining, lounging, and leisure activities.

When people go to the trouble of filling the area around the house with stylish furniture, potted plants, swimming pool, barbecue, even electric lights, it seems clear that the space is meant to be important in the family's life. To get the most out of the effort you put into creating it requires careful attention to detail.

Take care of the basics first. These include screening for privacy with trees and large shrubs and, if necessary, fences. Hide unsightly views with plantings and take into consideration that some plants will soon outgrow their present confines. Get help from a plant nursery and check in landscaping books before making selections of plants.

■

When you have a room with many windows, try selecting casual funiture. In this case, bamboo furniture and lots of plants create a space that is part indoor, part outdoor in feeling.

If you have lots of trees, don't feel you must keep every one. Undesirable trees, which are weedy or which compete with plantings, can be taken down. Opt for trees and shrubs that you like and, to minimize maintenance, that are known to be trouble-free and hardy in your area.

Where there are young children, choose a surface that's soft enough for safe play, yet solid enough for fast-moving games. Grass and wood decking both meet the need.

An important factor in the comfort level of your outdoor room is choosing a type of flooring that is

most suitable. Choice of surface should be based on local climatic conditions, the cost of upkeep in time as well as money, and the relationship between original cost and longevity. Select a surface that is in character with the house and the surrounding landscape. Consider whether the surface is unsightly or slippery after rain. Does it dry quickly? Will winter snows wash some of the surfacing away? Gravel and wood chips are inexpensive compared with other surfacing materials, but both need to be replenished frequently.

The most popular outdoor surfaces have been around long enough to prove itself in a wide variety of climates. Include the following in the category: brick, stone, wood decking, concrete blocks, poured concrete, and gravel. In some areas, tiles, beach pebbles, wood rounds, crushed rock, and indoor-outdoor carpeting in a grasslike texture are also popular.

When thinking about price, consider the cost of the labor to install it. For example, you could probably lay brick in sand a little at a time until the job is done. Poured concrete, on the other hand, is best done all at once.

An outdoor area for leisure and entertainment might include a sitting area, a dining spot, a child's play area, and a service area out of sight and smell. Plan outdoor spaces in relation to windows and doors to bring views of the garden into the home and to draw people into the outdoors.

It usually works best to locate a specific outdoor 'room' near the indoor room used for the same purpose. For example, if you locate the outdoor kitchen near its indoor counterpart, you will have easy access to food, drinks, and utensils. Entertaining a crowd near the living room will pose no noise problems. Locate a private outdoor space near the master bedroom where it's quiet and private. If the spaces were reversed, there would be access and noise problems.

A partial ceiling in the form of a canvas awning, wooden lattice, or fiberglass panels makes an area usable for a longer period of time and in bad weather. Shrubs, trees, and fences can also be used;

Courtesy of Brown Jordan

▪*LEFT:*
Dining outdoors is one of the most pleasant ways to enjoy a meal.

and a canopy of leaves overhanging part of the sitting area also serves as a shady enclosure in summer.

If you are near a street and want to obscure traffic noises, water is very helpful. A recirculating fountain whose flow can be increased to mask competing sounds is a wonderful idea. Of moderate benefit in counteracting street noises are plants with rustling leaves.

You can add to an outdoor area that is too small for your purposes and make the addition look as if it has always been there if you choose materials in keeping with what you already have. If you have a bluestone patio and a brick house, you can add a brick-edged bluestone extension. If you have a redwood deck, you can add more redwood and stain both parts so they match. After you've added the square footage, follow up with new plantings.

▪*OPPOSITE PAGE:*
You can create a great sense of enclosure with structures such as this. Nowadays, new textiles and fillings make it possible to have cushions that withstand rain.

The entryway

One of the most rewarding outdoor projects is redoing the front yard to make it more convenient and attractive. Not only does this improvement lift spirits, it also increases property value and contributes to safety.

The scope of the project can be as small as setting out planters or as large as a completely new planting, lighting, and walkway scheme. If improvements are called for, give your place a close inspection by strolling around the front of the house with pencil and pad to gather and record firsthand impressions. Armed with information on needed improvements, an individual must decide whether to tackle the job alone or hire a professional landscaper.

It is easy from the start to recognize a well-planned entry. There is a clear and obvious direction to the door that is immediately visible from the driveway. The path to the front door is wide enough for at least two people to walk side by side. The area directly in front of the door is large enough to accommodate four people.

Signs that a new approach is needed include overgrown or straggly shrubbery, narrow or broken walkways, and inadequate lighting. Watch out for potential danger spots such as slippery patches, which dripping water turns icy in cold weather, or cracks in the pavement, which could cause someone to trip. Lighting should illuminate the path and steps.

If it turns out that plantings are too large or unsightly or create cleanup problems by dropping branches, leaves, and unwanted fruits on the pathway, these can be replaced with plantings that require less maintenance.

Sources of help

Professional landscape designers and architects can help you solve landscaping problems in the same way that interior designers help you with interior spaces. Landscape designers plan and design outdoor surfaces and lighting as well as planting beds, and they can supervise their installation.

A designer can create a five- or ten-year plan that allows you to do things together in a series of related steps. For example, if lawn repair is desired and a lighting fixture will be installed on a pole in the lawn, it makes sense to first put the pole in and then do the lawn repair. If regrading the lawn is necessary and installation of a swimming pool is contemplated, delay the former until the latter is done. It gets all the messy business of earth moving out of the way at once, and a savings may be realized on the rental of large equipment and the labor, which can be very costly. Of course, the most important benefit of such an extended renovation plan is the distribution of the cost over time.

▪ *OPPOSITE PAGE:*
The brick, stone, shingles, and painted wood used in the construction of this patio will give excellent service over many years provided they are well maintained.

▪ *LEFT:*
Choose outdoor furniture that can withstand the elements for poolside dining. One excellent choice is heavy-duty wrought or cast aluminum.

ROOMS FOR REST AND REJUVENATION

The master bedroom

If there's a new trend in a room as timeless as the bedroom, it is the expansion of customary activities there. Rest, grooming, and storage remain the important basics. However, deskwork, exercising, watching television, and listening to music are increasingly centered in the bedroom. A survey taken in America by a mail-order retailer of bedding found that on average six hours a week is spent in the bedroom just listening to music.

The great variety of furnishings now geared to the bedroom makes it easy to turn it into a multipurpose room. Storage beds with headboards have built-in lights and large roll-out drawers beneath the mattress and box spring. Chaises, easy chairs, small refrigerators, portable stereos, and desks also are routinely used in a master bedroom.

There are some disadvantages in a bedroom that resembles a living room or study. Researchers have found that it is harder to fall asleep in a room cluttered with reminders of daytime activities. You can provide for multiple activities without compromising the quality of sleep by separating sleep and work areas. A bookcase or a screen can be placed so that there are two separate areas. Cut down on clutter by using the walls and unseen areas behind doors for storage and by placing some items in containers such as steamer trunks, storage cubes, or wicker baskets.

Increase a sense of peace by deadening annoying outside sounds with fabric and using window coverings to protect the room from the lights of passing cars and streetlights. Use an air conditioner, fan, portable heater, electric blanket, or down comforter to alleviate ventilation, heat, and cooling problems.

Choose a soft color scheme—pastels are favorites because they are soothing and flattering. Any colors that are not strident work well, however. Employ vibrant colors and bright patterns as accents.

A dramatic bed, such as a carved four-poster, an ornate brass bed, or one with an upholstered head-

■
In this bedroom, the windows are an appealing feature; the generous use of fabric gives them appropriate emphasis.

board, can become the room's centerpiece. Drape the bed with fabric. A dust ruffle and a matching or contrasting coverlet are a starting point. Use additional pillows to carry out the theme of soft luxury, covering them with fabric that coordinates with or matches the coverlet.

Don't allow lack of budget for a grand bed to stand in your way. You can drape any bed with fabric by building a framework with two-by-fours and then draping the structure with fabric. You can paint any type of bed with such motifs as lovebirds, flowers, ribbons, or trellises. Nail up trellis panels (available in garden-supply outlets) behind a bed that has no headboard. Paint the trellis and interweave silk flowers or paint the flowers and trellis directly on the wall as a *trompe l'oeil* scene. Not too

handy with a paintbrush? Hire an art student to execute your idea.

Opulent window treatments in a coordinating fabric carry out a luxurious tone. Layered treatments pairing substantial, solid or floral printed fabrics with sheers covering the windows themselves are attractive and functional. By coordinating fabrics in a bedroom, you eliminate some of the visual clutter in a bedroom yet end up with a room that is well decorated without having lots of elements.

While good reading lamps are essential for those who read in bed, mood lighting is also important. Control the amount of light with dimmers. For a soft complexion-enhancing reading light, cover bedside lamps with string shades in colors such as peach or lavender, or use pink-tinted light bulbs.

■

A dressing table is ideally located near natural light, as in this bedroom.

An easy chair, a chaise, or a slipper chair and personal accessories such as photos in silver or porcelain frames and silk flower arrangements are additional features that complete a romantic room.

The cheerfully cluttered look of a nineteenth-century English, American, or French boudoir can begin with a four-poster, one of the most popular beds. Unadorned, it contributes a solid sense of history. With the addition of bed hangings and extra pillows, it is a romantic cocoon. The idea is to have all your treasured things around you—books, magazines, writing paper, and so on. The look is particularly appealing to those who enjoy lots of different patterns together. While patterns can differ, they should relate in color or theme, and if the bed is the

room's focal point, don't go overboard in the window treatment. Keep it compatible but peaceful.

A fabric headboard with matching covers and cushions is a timeless look that can be used in both the master bedroom and a child's room. Once custom-made only, the look is more accessible today through furniture stores and fabric specialty stores. Some furniture manufacturers now make upholstered headboards as well as a range of coordinating products such as matching comforters, bedspreads, bed ruffles, cushions, and skirted dressing tables and chairs.

The selection of fabric, the shape of the headboard, the sewing details, and the upholstery treatment and trim are varied enough to turn the look

■

People are likely to be doing deskwork in the bedrooms so it's a good idea to include a place to work.

into either masculine or feminine, traditional or modern.

Choose fabric that doesn't easily show dirt. Eventually, any material will become shabby, but some will stand up longer. Consider having an extra slipcover made in a different material so that the look can be changed in the summer. The second cover also extends the life of the first headboard. Matching fabric treatments—say a bench at the bottom of the bed—can also be used.

A tall fabric headboard makes a complete picture by itself and can eliminate the need for wall decor behind the bed; it is an excellent foil for big, comfortable clusters of pillows that may overpower a standard-height headboard. There are few rules or restrictions with upholstery, other than to avoid an overcoordinated or fussy look that comes from too many frills and bows.

Storage
The practical aspects of storage in the bedroom usually involve refitting the closets to get more use out of the space you have. To maximize storage room, keep closet floors empty, placing shoes at eye level. When there are a number of shelves, make those on the bottom jut out and make the top shelves recede for easy reach. Store seldom-used items like suitcases and extra blankets on top shelves.

If you've got a room without a closet, perhaps it will be possible to gain a large amount of storage space by installing a 2-foot- (60-cm-) deep closet across the face of a wall. To compensate for cutting your room off, mirror the doors to create the illusion of greater depth.

If clutter is your biggest problem, minimize it by combining small items such as jewelry, hosiery, scarves, and shoes. Keep shoes in labeled boxes. Fold scarves up and place in a small set of transparent drawers on a closet shelf. You can also hang them on a kitchen mug rack nailed to the door or clip them to trouser hangers or clothespins on the crossbar of a hanger. Store stockings separately by color in clear plastic bags or in clear plastic shoe boxes. Store handbags flat, loosely stuffed with tissue paper.

To gain more room in a closet, rearrange it by adding several hanging bars at different heights. A center section of shelves makes it possible to double the amount of usable storage space.

■

A well-organized closet is a necessity these days. It is worthwhile to spend the money to make the closet attractive as well as functional since it's a space you will be looking at every day.

Children's bedrooms
Enough room to play and accessible storage bring order to the chaos of jumbled toys and projects. To add play space to the room, use the walls fully by installing wall-hugging furniture. A desk and shelves can be incorporated into a securely installed wall system.

The coming of age of the baby boom generation has produced a larger birthrate and a bumper crop of home furnishings geared to making children's rooms safer, more educational, and more fun. The new products include printed sheets, furniture, accessories, and wallpaper with an educational and a play component. Several companies, for example, make wallpaper with stick-on vinyl figures that can be removed and reapplied by a child playing a game. Different patterns are suited to different age

© Jennifer Levy

groups—toddlers through age twelve. Look for these products in wallpaper outlets. A great variety of decorative wallpaper borders are available ready-made.

When selecting from among all these items, consider function first. It is more cost-effective to purchase a storage piece such as a wall cabinet that a child can use through the teenage years than less expensive infant furniture that is soon outgrown.

Contemporary enameled metal furniture and plastic laminate covered pieces are durable and attractive. If a traditional look is preferred, scour antiques shops for bookcases, cabinets, desks, dressers, and beds in pine and oak. These older pieces are usually durable and well built. When stripped of dark finishes they are also fashionable.

Iron bedsteads, which can be painted white, are enjoying a renaissance, especially for little girls' rooms. Since they often come in odd sizes, measure before buying to make sure they will fit the standard 39- or 54-inch (100- or 137-cm) mattress. If they don't, you can either cut them down or order custom bedding, but, naturally, custom mattresses and sheets will add to the cost.

■

A child's bedroom is likely to be a play space as well as a sleeping space. This room offers an active child many opportunities for play.

© Phillip Ennis

■

Fanciful storage furniture is great fun. If you opt for this idea, try to select a design with longevity. After all, your child will probably be using the furniture for at least ten years, if not longer.

Surfaces

An idea that is easy on upkeep and inexpensive if you do it yourself is to paint the floor with enamel, stencil a pattern over it, and then seal the whole with a polyurethane finish.

Painted walls are often best, since the many colors and patterns of toys and children's artwork provide all the necessary color. Enamel paint is preferable to flat paint because it cleans more easily. Use long-lived colors, not baby colors, for most furniture and surfaces in a nursery. Fill in with easily changed children's accessories.

Upkeep

Blends of natural-fiber fabrics and synthetics require less maintenance. Fabrics such as stretch velours and terry cloth work well in infants' rooms since they launder well. For older children who are apt to track in all kinds of dirt, soil-release finishes may be helpful. Cotton polyester blends are good since they, too, are machine-washable and require little or no ironing.

Using patterned sheets or colorful printed fabrics, you can sew window treatments, bedding such as spreads, quilts, and quilt covers and dust ruffles.

Storage

For kids, you can outfit rooms and closets with ready-made organizers. These include toy-storage boxes, underbed boxes, clothes bags, chests of drawers, child-size hangers, and shelves. Some systems require attachment to the wall, but also look for freestanding closet organizers that can be removed when the child outgrows them.

Privacy may be a problem if you are outfitting a room for siblings to share. Dividers such as freestanding screens can be used to break up the space, or you might opt to hang blinds from the ceiling. These can be lowered or raised as necessary. Wall units backed with cork divide a room and solve storage problems at the same time.

Be ready to consider the unconventional when it comes to furniture. For example, if space is tight, think about trundle beds or bunk beds. Often they can be separated into two freestanding beds if a larger room becomes available.

Furniture shaped like cars or planes or trucks is popular now. But while these themed pieces are great fun and original, they do have one drawback: They'll need to be replaced when a child becomes an adolescent. Economy suggests choosing more lasting designs for the big pieces and allowing accessories and wallpaper borders, which are easily changed, to carry the special decorating message. Of course, if there are several children, the furniture can be passed along, but selecting white or neutral furniture allows you more flexibility in changing the room to accommodate the growing child.

For occasional overnight guests, futon mats, sofas or rugs on which a sleeping bag can be placed are all perfectly acceptable.

Safety

Safety is as important as decorative appeal in a child's room. Youthful exuberance demands extra protection from the rigors of play and occasional misuse of materials. Minimize potential problems by examining furniture and accessories carefully before buying and by installing them properly.

For example, solid-wood bunk beds are often sturdier than tubular metal or particleboard. Parents should remember that anything that can be climbed probably will be, so tall furniture is safer if it's attached to the wall. The guideline is that if the object could be dangerous when tipped over, secure it to the wall.

If you put a bunk bed in the corner, there will be two walls for support. Make sure the child will be able to climb up and down the bed ladder without slipping through the rungs. Tubular metal ladders can be slippery, especially if the child is wearing footed pajamas; and with children under four, a bed guard or partition on the exposed side of the upper berth is a good idea.

Children may find windows attractive surfaces to crawl on but there are several ways to protect them (the children) from the consequences of these actions, including placing a safety latch on the window so it can't open more than a few inches (cm) when the children are playing unsupervised. If the window is a large single pane, employ shatterproof glass, or if this is impossible, place wooden shutters at the bottom part to provide a barricade between the children and the glass. Another idea to take into consideration is to mount a grille or a few wooden dowels from left to right. These decorative trims can deter a ball or other projectile from hitting and breaking the window.

Be careful of exposed electric outlets in the room, especially when children are under the age of six. You can buy inexpensive plug-guards at a hardware store. They fit into the outlets. Other safety suggestions include eliminating floor lamps in a child's

© Design: Janice Gewirtz; Photo: Rick Albert

room, since they can topple over if a child gets caught in the cord. Track lighting and light fixtures are safer as a rule than freestanding lamps, especially since a child might very well consider a lamp a fascinating toy.

A toy chest with a removable cover or with a latch that keeps the lid open is safer than a toy chest with a heavy attached lid that can fall down and severely injure or even lock a child in. Check furniture and toy parts for any sharp edges, which can be protected against by covering them with putty or clay.

▪

Many teenagers enjoy sleeping in an unconventional room. This platform bed arrangement is a good use of space in a small room.

A pink, blue, and white scheme is sweet, yet not too juvenile. The antique desk, cabinet, and bedstead can be recycled as adult furniture. This room is timeless.

© Phillip Ennis

Whether to opt for a hard- or a soft-surface floor covering is primarily a comfort and care decision. Wall-to-wall carpeting is easy to maintain and comfortable underfoot and may help prevent skinned knees. Area rugs work well, too, especially if you have nice wood floors. A good choice if you're seeking an area rug is a washable bathmat with a no-skid backing.

When deciding on how to decorate a child's room, bear in mind that even young children of two and three can take part in decorating their own room.

"Kids treat their room with respect when they've had a say in decorating it," according to Antonio F. Torrice, a designer who specializes in decorating for children at home and in public facilities.

Not only will family fights diminish, but your offspring will develop more self-esteem if they have a say in room arrangement and colors, he says. When you give children a choice, you teach them that they can influence their environment, a powerful learning experience that builds self-esteem, according to Torrice, who deplores the practice of furnishing a child's room to satisfy the parent's long-cherished dreams. Instead, when called in—usually by parents with liberal ideas—he engages his young client in game-playing and conversation to learn how the child wants the space arranged and what his or her color preferences are.

It doesn't have to cost more to do things this way, because there is an inexpensive as well as an expensive way to provide for the communications, self-expression, and storage centers Torrice says should be part of every child's space.

A simple chalkboard or an intercom permit parents and kids to leave messages for one another. Self-expression can be encouraged lavishly with track lighting, a microphone, and a custom-built stage or modestly, by substituting a curtain with windows in it for the closet door. Accessible storage can be custom-made or discount-store plastic basins with hand-lettered labels on a wooden shelf.

Low-cost window shades can be installed to pull up rather than down so a child can operate them and thus gain a sense of mastery.

Courtesy of Lillian Vernon Corp.

Letting children decorate their rooms

■ Allow your child to pick a color he or she wants and put it into the room in some way—through paint, sheets, a bedspread, or even a desk blotter.

■ Rearrange the room to make all or most of the storage area accessible at child height. Some suggestions are to lower the rod in the closet, to substitute more manageable hardware for children to grasp, and to label containers to help children know where things are. Enlist the child's suggestions for where and how to store items.

■ Incorporate learning centers in the room that reflect your child's special interests. If he is fascinated by weather forecasting, hang a thermometer by the window. If she likes to collect leaves or rocks, provide a little magnifying glass and a place to display finds.

■ Rehang art, clocks, and bulletin boards closer to a child's eye level.

The nursery

You can create a first nursery with a minimum of cash by substituting a major investment of ingenuity and do-it-yourself labor. To lower costs in the nursery, consider these points:

It's less expensive to paint than to paper the baby's room. Paint is easier to change as the child grows older. For decorative impact, paint and then buy a 12-inch- (30-cm-) wide strippable wallpaper border and place on the wall at chair-rail height so the baby can see and enjoy it. Shop for wallpaper seconds to keep costs down.

Shop for baby furniture at flea markets and yard sales. Check in the classified pages of the daily newspaper to find the sales. A scrubdown with detergent and water followed by a repainting will sanitize and freshen painted furniture. Wood finishes can be refinished at home fairly easily using products that are available at paint and hardware stores.

Choose bright colors for walls and accessories instead of the traditional pale pastels. Bright colors stimulate an infant and help in the development of alertness. Choose two main colors and use them throughout the room for walls, bed linen, upholstery fabric, and accessories. Some lively schemes are light blue and white with red accents, grass green and yellow with pink and white accents, navy blue and white with red or yellow accents.

Don't overspend on lighting. Bright white light has been shown to annoy infants. Instead, use small table lamps bought secondhand and repainted to match the decor. Place lamps on dressers or corner tables out of the baby's grasp. Make lampshades by gluing patterned sheeting, leftover wallpaper or borders, or other colorful material onto inexpensive paper shades. The fabric shade can coordinate with sheets or other fabrics in the room.

If there is no room for a separate nursery, you can craft a room divider out of a 4-by-8-foot (1.3-by-2.6-m) piece of plywood. Decorate one side with bright pictures and photos to catch the baby's eye. A paneled screen or a bookcase can be used to divide space temporarily.

■

The zoned arrangement of this long, skinny bathroom is an efficient use of space; in addition, the use of white, with black accents, creates the illusion of greater space.

BATHROOMS

It's curious that the smallest (and unfortunately often the most inconvenient and least attractive) room in the house should be also one of the most utilized. The bathroom is one of the first stops in the morning and the last at night for everyone in the household as well as a frequent resort during the day. Time and money spent to equip it to meet the household's requirements almost always is amply repaid in comfort.

Much in this room is preordained and difficult to change, so if you are planning a new bath or engaging in remodeling, be sure to build for the future, considering how the room would need to function if the size of the household were increased or a physically impaired person had to use it. It even helps to consider the possible needs of people you don't know, since the condition of the bathrooms is a major factor in the marketability of a residence.

For many, a single bath functions for both family and guests. The special needs of young children, teenagers, and guests all must be fitted into a room only a little bigger than a good-size broom closet.

If you have space enough for several bathrooms, the specific requirements of those who will use them can be considered more closely. A master bath, for example, might have room for a lighted makeup center, a full-length mirror, exercise equipment, and an oversize whirlpool tub, or spa bath. A children's bath could have a sink at a lower height to accommodate youngsters, hampers for soiled clothes and wet towels, and storage for bath toys. A powder room could be a tiny decorative delight with special wallpaper and a painted china sink.

However, all baths share some common requirements. Before finalizing decisions on materials and arrangement, consider how your choices meet the following criteria:

- ■ Efficient appliances
- ■ Ventilation
- ■ Light
- ■ Safety
- ■ Durable surfaces
- ■ Privacy
- ■ Comfort

Each household has its own needs in relation to the bathroom, so it is helpful to have specific information about your requirements when remodeling or planning a new bath. A good way to get this data is to map the daily routine. By making a list of items stored in the room and specific activities that require electric outlets and storage space, you gain a clear vision of how the room is being used.

Dual mirrors and dual basins are worthwhile additions to a bathroom.

■ *RIGHT:*

Although marble is a costly luxury material, it offers longevity and, of course, beauty.

■ *FAR RIGHT:*

A large bathroom like this can be fitted with extra drawers and closets.

Another aspect of your research is to consider the ways in which the space you have now is not meeting the household's needs. The two parts together allow you to use design to make improvements.

If the evidence shows it's warranted, perhaps a second bath can be added. If that isn't possible, maybe a double basin would relieve the congestion that is inevitable if several people have to use the room at the same time every morning. A larger area for storage, a locked cabinet for prescription drugs, a better light, more towel bars or a new location for them, removing the toilet to a separate alcove, installing grab bars in the tub: These are some choices that can make a difference in efficiency and convenience and safety.

Storage

Storage space is one of the most important and frequently unmet needs in the bath. Because they waste precious storage space, pedestal sinks are a less effective choice than a built-in sink surrounded by cabinet space. You will be more likely to have enough storage space of the right size and depth if you have analyzed your needs and gone to the

trouble of measuring the bulkier items you'll be keeping in the bathroom. Installing a shelf that is 2 inches (5 cm) too shallow and 3 inches (7.5 cm) too short to accommodate the necessary stacks of towels is a preventable mishap.

Open shelving or closed? Both effectively handle the clutter. Chances are you'll have a preference

based on your personal style and perhaps the other occupants' attitudes toward folding and putting away. An advantage of open shelving is that it takes up less room. If space saving is a must but closed shelving is preferable, consider installing a blind, shade, or curtain to hide the mess on a temporary basis.

Before investing in custom cabinetry, visit the best bath shop you can find. The array of plastic towel bars, soap dishes, toothbrush holders, storage utensils, and freestanding cabinets is growing all the time. You may be able to buy what you need ready-made without going to the expense of having a cabinet built.

Fixtures

The physical and psychic benefits of water are now well known. Whirlpools with multiple jets and aerated "soft water" sprays that break like bubbles on the skin have become the bath of choice in the United States and elsewhere. New types of faucets are among the most recent products. The most dramatic is a flume spout that is open at the top so that the water courses out in a wave or waterfall.

The variety of fixtures and faucets ranges from ultramodern in looks to antique. Decorative products that function for today but look like their late-

© Phillip Ennis

BELOW:
Creative lighting solutions in the bathroom focus on using light in decorative as well as functional ways.

Courtesy of American Standard

■*ABOVE:*
The addition of an elegant sink like this one would enliven any bathroom.

nineteenth-century and early-twentieth-century antecedents make it feasible to decorate for an old-time look without sacrificing new technology. When authenticity is everything, you can buy old fixtures from retailers who specialize in architectural antiques.

The placement of plumbing components also governs their serviceability. For example, many pedestal sinks are installed 6 inches (15 cm) too low, says American human-motion authority Alexander Kira, who has studied the physical motions associated with bathing and toilet activities. A height of 34 to 36 inches (86 to 92 cm) is best, and faucets in the bathroom basin should release the water to the middle of the sink, not against the back. Also, most people prefer a single spigot.

Safety

Slippery materials, inaccessible controls, and patterned tiles that disguise obstacles such as steps or changes in level lead to bathroom accidents that could be avoided by more safety-conscious decorating decisions.

For floors, use nonskid materials such as tile with a rough texture, carpet, or a rug with nonskid backing. New tubs come with nonslip bottoms. An old one can be fitted with adhesive strips or a rubber mat. If possible, tub controls should be placed so bathwater can be turned on without getting in (to guard against scalding).

The safest way to get in and out of the tub is to sit on the edge and swing your feet over, holding onto grab bars. Any installation that makes this proce-

Choosing a whirlpool or spa bath

Manufacturers report that a whirlpool tub or spa bath is the most desired bath fixture. While some are oversize, smaller models fit into standard tub spaces no larger than 5 feet (1.7 m) long. Besides fit, another concern is the tub's weight. Materials such as fiberglass and acrylic are light, and acrylic can be molded into a variety of shapes, such as a corner tub, fairly easily. Manufacturers also are working with other new materials, which reduce weight and permit variation in shapes at reasonable cost. When choosing a whirlpool or spa bath, seek certification that the tub is safe.

The tub's weight when full of water may be a critical factor if installation will be on an upper floor of an old house. If this is a concern, select one of the lighter-weight acrylic tubs. Even if you have room for a very large whirlpool, you may not want it. The size of tub selected should be geared to the capacity of

the hot-water heater, which should supply three-quarters of the water capacity of the bathtub.

You will find the tub's vital statistics on the label. The specs give you the tub's length, width, and depth, number of water jets (from four to six for a one-user model, six to eight for two-person tubs), the water capacity, and the combined weight of tub and water.

Some models have jets that are individually adjustable. Most people prefer to be able to change the direction of flow to fit their own body. Some units offer a feature that permits more aeration of the water for more bubbles. Placement of controls can be on the tub or on the wall. The most popular option, according to one manufacturer, is to have the controls on the tub itself, but wall-mounted controls might be preferable for either functional or decorative reasons.

■*ABOVE:*
This glassed-in shower has the added feature of a seat.

■ *LEFT:*
Whirlpool baths have become the most desired upgrade in the bath. A home spa large enough to be used for exercise and relaxation represents another step up.

■ *BELOW:*
A graceful faucet like this one would add charm to even the most common bathroom design.

Colors Provence II, Sandpiper Studios

■*ABOVE:*

A modest bathroom has been given a new look with wallpaper and a fabric skirt for the sink. Accessories such as an interesting plantstand also add to the charm.

■*ABOVE, RIGHT:*

The use of an unusually deep wallpaper border adds great distinction to this bath. A black-and-white color scheme provides strong graphic interest.

dure impossible has the potential to be unsafe. Grab bars should be installed in tubs—the towel bar is not strong enough to support the full weight of an adult—and handrails on platform tubs. If you've decided on a large sunken tub, make sure the controls are placed so you can turn on the faucet, check the water temperature, and clean the tub without having to get into it.

The best arrangement for bathing is a separate shower and bathtub because the optimum configuration is different for each. A good soaking tub is contoured to support the back in comfort while the best shower has a flat bottom and, ideally, a seat. In a stall shower, the user should be able to get out of the stream of water, and controls for the water should be at the point of entry while the flow of water is directed to the opposite wall to minimize the danger of scalding.

The path to the toilet, which often is used at night under poor light, should be clear. Remove obstacles,

such as hampers, standing towel racks, or slippery area rugs, and never place a toilet on a platform. In fact, it's safer to completely avoid all changes in floor level in a bathroom, even though these dramatic design devices are currently fashionable, especially in luxury master baths.

To minimize the hazards of excessively hot or cold water in the bathtub or sink, place governors on faucets to automatically mix cold and hot water if you have separate faucets. The device is inexpensive and easy to install.

Decorating options

Counter materials are a way to customize bath decor. The luxury surfaces of marble, granite, and tile and more affordable plastic laminate in white or colors or patterns have been augmented by a number of newer synthetics, such as cultured onyx and cultured marble.

Other decorative products specifically for the bath or highly adaptable to it include water-

■
Consider a mural for the upper walls of a bath that is tiled three quarters of the way. Such a treatment conveys unique distinction when well executed.

resistant vinyl wall coverings, decorative bath collections that coordinate fabrics and wall coverings, and even tile that matches the plumbing fixtures. Tie-ins between tile companies and bath-fixture companies have made it possible to buy fixtures and tiles with the same design details. Ceramics craftsmen can easily produce custom tiles, so the same idea can be carried out by individuals. However,

bath fixtures are usually installed for a very long time, so a conservative design approach is usually the best policy.

If you want to refurbish the bath without actually replacing fixtures or moving them, a facelift can be accomplished with new wall coverings or paint, a new set of towels, and matching or coordinated shower curtain and window covering.

WORK SPACES

■

An attractive, efficient kitchen is the result of careful space planning and personalization.

AN EFFICIENT KITCHEN

You can have an attractive and efficient kitchen in almost any amount of space and in arrangements that run the gamut from single-wall, corridor, L-shaped, or U-shaped to four-wall arrangements of appliances, cabinets, and counters.

The trick is to organize your space to minimize the steps between sink, stove, refrigerator, and storage areas and to provide easy access to each from any point. Space planning comes first, well before selection of kitchen style and cabinetry, surface materials, and appliance brands. As you will soon learn, the products come in standard sizes and shapes, so you are sure to find a style you like once you've worked out the functional arrangement of the room.

Studies of how people actually work in their kitchen have resulted in adoption of three basic principles of efficient kitchen planning:

■ Storing items where they will be needed first
■ Personalizing arrangements to the physical needs of the primary user
■ Organizing the kitchen into work centers

Storage

Although at first thought it might make sense to store all fabrics, all paper goods, and all dishes together, it's actually more efficient to break up these large categories into smaller ones based on where you will be using the item. It is convenient to have clean dish towels next to the sink and place-mats next to the dining table. Paper towels belong near the sink, but paper napkins are handier near the table. The good china used only for special occasions does fine in the dining room but everyday china is best kept near the kitchen table. Analyze your actual working patterns before settling on where to store frequently used items.

Personalization

Many choices of cabinet arrangements and hardware are available. Counter heights, though standard at 36 inches (92 cm), can be lowered or raised an inch or two.

Work Centers

A work center consists of a major appliance and the counter and storage space near it. Motion studies show the sink center is the most frequently used. Choose a central place for the sink and surrounding area and make sure it's convenient to both the refrigerator and stove since it's usually a way station between them. As a rule, a dishwasher is located next to the sink, if this appliance is part of the set-up. If more than one person normally prepares a meal or uses the kitchen at the same time, consider a double sink, which is also useful if you do not have a dishwasher. Diagonal siting of the kitchen sink has become popular recently in custom kitchens. Angling a sink may waste a little space, but it softens the squareness of the room and creates visual interest. Placing the sink in a corner creates a large food preparation area to the right and left of it.

The natural beauty of earth tones and wooden cabinets combine to give this wet bar a warm, luxurious look.

As kitchens grow larger, additional centers may need to be installed to accommodate dishes, linens, and other accessories.

The centerpiece of the range area is the cooktop and ovens. Allow enough storage space for pots and pans. Use heatproof material such as ceramic, metal, or natural stone on the part of the counter next to the range so that hot pots can be left there for a moment. This feature is even more useful next to a wall oven since you'll need a place to rest a heavy, hot roasting pan. Install a vented hood or an exhaust fan to remove both heat and cooking odors before they permeate the house. There should be a clear path from the range to the dining table.

The area around the refrigerator should include storage space for clean containers. The refrigerator door should open away from the counter.

Besides these stations, you also need an uninterrupted counter where you can assemble the ingredients for dishes, use small appliances such as food processors and electric mixers, grind coffee, roll out pastry, arrange platters, and so on. Adequate electric outlets and handy storage space for small appliances to be placed comfortably, not to create an eyesore, are two essentials. Choose a countertop that accommodates food preparation and can be scrubbed clean so it is sanitary.

As kitchens grow larger and become more elaborate, additional centers may be installed. Some of the common centers include a serving area where dishes, glasses, flatware, linens, and accessories are stored; a food-storage pantry; a spot for a microwave oven where snacks can be prepared, a cleaning center where appliances and cleaning supplies are stored; and a home office, planning, and message center. If you have a large household, a secondary sink or cooking area may be a useful, if not necessary, luxury. A table or counter for dining is also an important part of most kitchens if you do intend to dine in the kitchen. Some families opt not to dine there.

Before embarking on kitchen remodeling plans, mentally walk through the kitchen you have and review the stages of meal preparation. This exercise should disclose flaws and strengths. If the room arrangement is satisfactory, a facelift, which is the least expensive project, may be all that's needed. This might involve new cabinet fronts and hardware, better lighting, a new paint job, or wallpaper and a new floor.

Whether it's a renovation or a complete reworking, pay attention to the flow of activity around getting a meal ready. Bottlenecks that might be corrected quite easily in the planning stages can become extremely annoying: refrigerator doors that open into walls, wall ovens that are mounted too high to be considered safe, lack of counter space where it is needed, and intrusive center islands that block traffic.

Popular fads are not always desirable once you've analyzed how things actually work. Professional ranges and refrigerators—a supposed plus—can present problems in home kitchens, since they often require special ventilation, plumbing, or utility lines. If you are sure you would like professional equipment in your kitchen, look into the possibility of buying it used; schools, churches and other institutions often sell old appliances of this quality.

■

This modern country kitchen benefits from the use of modern materials and equipment, yet retains its original charm through its cheerful display of copper pots.

■

Wood floors do not easily show dirt, are resilient enough to withstand considerable use, and are comfortable on your feet.

Kitchen surfaces

Durable surfaces for kitchen counters, floors, walls, and cabinets are crucial for safety, efficiency, and comfort. You'll spend many hours using them and maintaining their good looks and cleanliness, so select the colors and patterns you can work comfortably around and think you can live with for a long time.

Many people prefer them, but natural materials are not innately superior. Synthetics score high in durability and good looks. In truth, no material is perfect for everyone, but many are perfect for someone. Coming up with the right selection is a matter of considering the budget, the working habits of those who will use the kitchen, and the degree of upkeep you're willing to assume.

Signs of age are ultimately unavoidable, but some materials, such as granite and laminates, look newer longer. Others, such as soapstone sinks, marble counters, and butcher block, age visibly, but in ways that many people find visually appealing. Marble, for example, can become more interesting as it dulls and discolors. Unlacquered brass and stainless steel acquire a patina as they age.

A particular quality can be both a plus and a minus. The same hardness that makes granite the ''rock of ages'' and allows it to keep its shine indefinitely also makes it more expensive to fabricate and imparts a formal and cold quality to rooms in which it's used extensively. Both granite and marble are excellent surfaces for preparing dough. Marble is softer and warmer than granite, but it needs more maintenance. It will stain and lose its shine.

Oak flooring has a grain so tight that it is difficult to stain it evenly. The problem becomes a virtue if you create a tortoise-shell finish by partially staining the oak black. Where the grain is most dense, the stain won't penetrate, leading to an interesting mottled effect.

Before choosing a surfacing material, make sure you understand its full range of attributes. Take stainless steel, for example. You can put hot pots on it, and it can be fabricated as a seamless countertop. That makes it versatile and sanitary. It's inexpensive as both a countertop and a sink material. It shows watermarks and fingerprints and scratches and it can be a noisy surface.

Butcher block's appeal is the warmth the natural wood imparts to the room. If you select an inch-and-a-half (3.8-cm) thickness, you can cut into it for two or three decades without getting anywhere near to pitting it. The upkeep for butcher block involves stripping off stains with steel wool and refinishing with a nontoxic oil.

Plastic laminate is an easy-maintenance material. It has good heat resistance and can be ordered in many colors and textures. It's difficult to disguise a scratch or chip.

Tile is highly decorative, especially for backsplashes, walls, and floors where its many designs can be used to create interesting patterns and its unevenness is not a drawback.

Brick floors look great but are uneven and hard to maintain. Rubber floors get scuffed easily, especially when they are in a solid color. Stone floors are costly, cold, and indestructible. Vinyl for floors not only comes in many patterns and in both tiles and rolled goods, but is serviceable and moderate in price. Wood floors are unorthodox in a kitchen. But if properly sealed, they don't show the dirt and they are comfortable floors—resilient enough to withstand dropped pots and easy on the feet.

■

Granite makes an excellent floor or counter surface and requires very little maintenance.

Cabinetry

Traditional wood cabinetry or the sleek look of European-style laminate cabinets? Both look great. About 60 percent of the average kitchen's cost is in the cabinets, so a worthwhile way to save money is with less expensive cabinetry.

Quality features you probably don't want to give up are doweled and glued construction, side-mounted drawer guides, and self-closing hinges. Attributes to look for are adjustable upper shelves, and base shelves that roll out to give you access to the back as well as the front. You'll need to be able to remove stains from cabinet surfaces, so make sure the finish is easy to clean.

The least expensive kitchen cabinets are mass-produced stock units (often carried by home-supply chains). They come in standard sizes, styles, and finishes. Locally made cabinets usually offer more

flexibility in size and custom storage options. Brand-name custom cabinets fabricated to order by major manufacturers offer the greatest number of sizes, interior storage aids, and finishes. They are also the most expensive. Custom details that add to both cost and convenience include wire baskets for vegetable storage, revolving lazy Susans for use in corner cabinets, full-length pantries with multiple swing-out shelves, bottle and tray storage centers, and appliance garages that hide small appliances behind closed doors at the rear of a counter.

With a little ingenuity, it's possible to use stock cabinetry for a custom installation. For example, instead of a ready-made floor-to-ceiling pantry, try stacking one stock base cabinet on top of another to make your own pantry. Use the base cabinet with drawers right side up on the bottom. Then top it with a two-door base cabinet that has been turned upside down with its toe-kick space removed. Since base cabinets are deeper than top cabinets, you can get more canned goods and staples into one of them than you would into an above-counter cabinet and a base unit.

If there is still room at the ceiling after the two cabinets have been installed, use the open space to hold attractive but rarely used serving dishes, salad bowls, and oversize baskets. If your stock cabinets go almost to the ceiling but not quite, you can install molding to hide the edges and have a built-in look rather than paying extra for custom sizes.

When you need more cabinetry but don't have any more wall space, perhaps you can create a storage divider or island between a dining area and the working part of the kitchen, or you could remove the dining table and substitute a combination eating and storage island where the table was. Storage cabinets can be the base with a laminate or butcher-block top that extends far enough beyond the base cabinet for stools. A 42-inch (107-cm) height can screen a work area from view.

For a highly decorative way of storing staples, purchase a 15-by-30-inch (38-by-76-cm) or 18-by-30-inch (45-by-76-cm) glass door cabinet. Turn it on its side and the glass door will now open out and down. It can be fitted with side-opening containers in which you store staples such as sugar and flour.

To gain more storage space for narrow items, recover the wasted space between the studs. This readily available space, which is about 3.5 inches (9 cm) deep, is behind your plasterboard walls and can be exposed and then painted or lined with patterned adhesive-backed plastic to house spices, canned goods, glasses, and other skinny items.

If you don't want to eliminate a window but it's keeping you from installing a needed storage cabinet, consider putting glass shelves in front of the window. Then place items such as glasses on the shelves so that the light and view are diffused but not altogether obscured. If a window is too low and you want to put a counter in front of it, cut out the counter in front of the window so that a narrow well is created. Use the well to hold growing herbs or other plants.

Style variations

Although you can have an efficient kitchen in virtually any style, there is one sense in which style and function are related. Some people work best in a setting of almost clinical efficiency. Others are more comfortable and effective in a softer, more cluttered setting. Know your style before you choose between a let-it-all-hang-out atmosphere and a clear-the-decks laboratory environment.

©Daniel Eifert, Design: Kate Altman

■ABOVE, LEFT:
The small space in this kitchen is used efficiently; notice the wall grid and ample shelf space.

■ABOVE, RIGHT:
This kitchen is perfectly organized: there is plenty of counter and shelf space; the dishwasher is near the sink, and the oven is near the window; and there are no obstructions in the work triangle from sink to refrigerator to oven.

Kitchen design checklist

■ Plan for counter space adjacent to the range, oven, sink, and dishwasher.
■ Locate dishwasher close to the sink.
■ Allow enough legroom under counters, peninsulas, and bars if you plan to use them for dining.
■ Place ovens at eye level or below for safety and provide a heatproof spot on the counter for hot pots and pans.
■ Aisles should be wide enough for two people to pass; there should be no need for household traffic to pass through the work triangle between stove, sink, and refrigerator.

Although some trends, such as a move towards natural materials in the kitchen, transcend national borders, color and cabinetry selections often are related to climate, geography, and culture. What's considered beautiful or stylish in materials thus changes according to region. Light woods, which are traditional in Scandinavian countries, for example, are often preferred in the American Midwest where many Scandinavians settled.

There is a practical aspect to preferences, too. In places with a cold winter, people often choose warm colors and wood cabinetry because they visually warm up the room. In southern climates where the living may be easy, easy-care laminates in light colors are preferred. Ceramic tile, a characteristic material in hot climates, is a good choice for floors and countertops because it is cool to the touch.

The advantages of a large, open kitchen-sitting area and dining area apply to many locales and

living styles. When there are young children at home, a large kitchen encourages family interaction and is good for a parent who needs to keep track of kids. It also offers enough room to store all the food, utensils, and appliances that people have these days and provides space in which to entertain informally.

A large kitchen, of course, has to be subdivided for efficiency and warmth. A rule of thumb is that the cumulative walking distance between the refrigerator, stove and sink should be no more than 21 feet (6.4 m), give or take a few inches (cm). A movable partition, a pass-through, hanging storage cabinets, or an island can serve as an effective divider. You can create a feeling of separation by lowering the ceiling in one area or changing the floor covering.

■

If you have the appropriate space, an eat-in kitchen is a worthwhile luxury—the chef always likes to have company.

Bright ideas

If a professional kitchen designer came to visit your house, what guidance would you receive? A recent survey of American kitchen designers says the biggest drawbacks to American kitchens are inadequate countertops, lack of storage space, outdated or broken appliances, and out-of-date cabinets.

New appliances their clients desire include a dishwasher (98 percent insisted on one), a microwave oven, a range with a grill, better lighting, and laundry equipment in or near the kitchen.

Features most people like are tile inserts in countertops both as a resting spot for hot pots and a decorative feature, roll-out shelves, oversize drawers for linen storage, a desk for paperwork, a large pantry, appliance garages to keep small electrics handy but out of sight, and open storage for nice-looking pots and gadgets to add a cozy country ambience.

Circular countertops and layouts with rounded edges give kitchens a softer flowing feeling. Bookcases for cookbooks, magazine racks, posters on walls, plants, and collectibles on shelves are special decorative touches that often appeal.

A kitchen facelift

Lack of budget for a major renovation doesn't have to sentence you to an unsatisfactory and ugly kitchen. Attack the biggest problem area first. If it's cabinet doors that for some reason cannot be stripped, sanded, and restained, then either replace them or paint them. A faux finish such as color washing can disguise surface imperfections. Change cabinet hardware after the surface has been tended to for a finished look.

Replace pitted, dirty, or dingy countertops. Plastic laminate or butcher block are relatively inexpensive. The newer synthetics such as Corian are somewhat more costly. For more storage capacity without new cabinets, refit existing cabinetry and drawers with aftermarket space expanders. Wire shelves and bins, lazy Susans, and lid holders can reclaim wasted space.

Treat walls to new wallpaper or a new paint job. A stenciled design gives a fresh look. Refinish old

© Melabee Miller/Envision

■ *FAR LEFT:*
Circular countertops and layouts with rounded edges can give a kitchen a soft, flowing feeling.

■ *ABOVE:*
This country kitchen, with its copper-stenciled refrigerator door, makes for a great conversation piece.

wood flooring or lay a new vinyl floor in a pattern such as a checkerboard or a bordered solid. Add undercabinet lighting if it's missing for a moderate expense and a big payback in comfort and efficiency.

Safety

Some specific recommendations have come from recent studies of how and where kitchen accidents occur. It's now suggested that cooktops and stoves have controls at the front and staggered burners, so it's not necessary to reach over hot pans and burners. Substitute side-by-side refrigerator-freezers for the top and bottom type, especially if anyone in the household has impaired mobility and difficulty in lifting and carrying.

Replace wobbly pots and pans and get a whistling teakettle to avoid the danger of pots that boil dry. Look for automatic shut-off features in small appliances such as toasters and irons.

Make sure that lighting levels are adequate to minimize the danger of accidents in the kitchen. Light should illuminate the work surface. Be aware of the patterns of light as daylight ebbs so you don't light the main work centers in such a way that for part of the day you are standing in your own shadow.

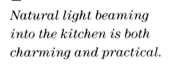

Natural light beaming into the kitchen is both charming and practical.

© Jennifer Levy

A kitchen that does everything but eat

Voice-activated appliances, a revolving pantry, a garbage recycling system, and a computerized scale that not only weighs you but also puts you on a diet if necessary are potential kitchen features of the future. They were all part of a kitchen by Eric Bernard in the Kips Bay Showhouse in New York City.

The stark yet luxurious black-and-white room had an inlaid marble floor and a range hood that looked like a pipe organ in a room designed "to make people in tuxedos look good," in the words of the designer who claimed it would cost more than $200,000 to duplicate the 14-by-28-foot (4-by-8-m) room. While the design was stunning—black granite counters, rounded white laminate cabinetry, smoked glass doors, glass domed ceilings, and black-and-white Italian tile floors—the technology seems even more startling. The kitchen showed off such newish appliances as a glass-front oversize refrigerator, an electrified revolving pantry, which, like the old manually operated dumbwaiter, brings the package to you instead of the other way around. A computer stores a cache of recipes and menus and generates shopping lists. An audiovisual system screens cooking videos.

The voice-activated system could be programmed to recognize up to four voices and to respond to voice commands to turn lights and television on and off, and start and stop the toaster, coffee maker, and food processor, and start the pantry shelves moving.

The waste disposal system was designed so four chutes delivered paper, plastic, aluminum, and other trash to separate containers in the basement for recycling.

Both photos courtesy of Gura Public Relations

Both photos courtesy of Gura Public Relations

■ *LEFT:*
This stunning design shows off the black granite counters, smoked-glass doors, black-and-white Italian tile floors, and white laminate cabinetry.

■ *ABOVE, LEFT:*
The technology here goes far beyond that of your average kitchen. A computer stores recipes and menus, and an audio/ video system screens cooking videos.

THE LAUNDRY ROOM

When a home laundry had to accommodate unwieldy equipment such as a mangle, nonelectric irons, and scrub boards, the basement was the best place for it. Modern equipment and permanent-press fabrics have started a laundry room revolution. These days, almost any room can be a laundry room. Some of the most common locations—each of which has its advantages—are the bathroom, a bedroom, a hallway near the bedrooms, the kitchen, the pantry, the family room, the utility room, any convenient closet, a basement workshop, a breezeway, or an attached garage.

An accessible spot for the laundry makes it easy to do quickly. Whether it is on the main floor or in the basement depends on the space available and the habits of the household. In or adjacent to the bathroom is a favorite location because it's near the place where so much soiled laundry accumulates. A family bath is usually near the bedrooms, too, another site of maximum accumulation.

The most convenient location may cost more to fit out but will make up for the high expense in convenience and time saved. If water and power access are handy, a new laundry room can be installed at moderate cost.

According to equipment manufacturers, a luxuriously efficient home laundry has all or most of these basics: counter space for folding and sorting; a sink for pretreating spots and stains; a hanging bar for permanent-press and freshly ironed clothes; hampers for colored and white things; an ironing board; storage space for cleaning products; and a container (possibly on wheels) to move clothes from one part of the house to another.

A subsidiary goal that is quite important to some people is to have a laundry room that is attractive enough to be cheerful and large enough to be uncramped. Those who have a hobby that creates a need for a deep sink and running water (houseplant enthusiasts, flower arrangers, water colorists, and enthusiasts of batik dyeing or candlemaking, for example) often find the laundry area a convenient place to locate facilities for these hobbies.

Ideas for laundries

Install a shower stall with a low faucet and hose attachment in a laundry room. It's an excellent spot to drip-dry clothes, drain wet umbrellas and rain coats, rinse off muddy boots, and shower houseplants.

A 6-foot-(2-m) long wall that can accommodate a depth of 30 inches (76 cm) has room for a washer and dryer and an 18-inch (45-cm) sink for pretreating fabrics and presoaking items. If there's another 18 inches (45 cm) or 2 feet (60 cm), add a closet to hang freshly ironed clothes and store detergents. Store the ironing board on the door. Conceal the working laundry behind bifold doors. Place a shelf above the equipment for additional supplies.

Add a greenhouse laundry room to the rear or side of an entryway. Use one side of the space for a space-saving stacked washer and dryer and the other side for a plant bench. Keep potting soil in a plastic garbage can under the plant bench. Roof and side vents keep the space cool in summer. Double glazing keeps it warm in winter.

Choosing a laundry location

Answer the following questions to arrive at the best location for a washer and dryer in your household.

▪ Where does laundry accumulate (bedrooms, bathrooms, exercise area)?

▪ When do you have time to do laundry (weekends, before work, after work, late evening)?

▪ Are there peripheral activities connected with laundry (ironing, sewing and mending, plant care, household repairs, hobbies)?

▪ Technical considerations: Is water handy from an already existing source such as bath or kitchen? Is drain access available? Is plumbing vent available?

■

The basic necessities for an efficient laundry room include a sink, hamper, ironing board, storage space, and a lot of counter space.

For a stylish basement laundry and exercise room, use black rubber flooring, white appliances, and cream-colored carpeted area for floor work in front of a full-length mirror. A wall-mounted television and music-playing equipment are accessible from a stationary exercise bike.

Centralize all aspects of household planning in a single room that includes laundry equipment. A prize-winning laundry occupying a room measuring 14 square feet (1.3 sq m), for example, accommodates a home office and room for sewing and ironing. There's a cork bulletin board along one wall, and a plastic-laminate desk surface stretches 9 feet (3 m) and provides facilities for organizing all aspects of the home. The laundry area includes a double sink with undercabinet lighting. Flower-arranging supplies as well as a cabinet for hanging permanent-press garments are also provided. One of the owner's favorite details is a shelf under the sink that holds a very large detergent box with a cup inside. The box need be lifted only once, when brought into the home.

THE HOME OFFICE

If you need a home office, but don't have room for a self-contained space, use part of another room. An alcove or a corner is a good spot. You can, however, create a feeling of separateness even in the main part of the room with changes in surface materials or screening. A different type of floor covering, paint, or wallpaper sets the office area apart. A paneled screen, cabinet, or group of tall plants also can camouflage the office.

In a house with two floors, the upstairs hallway can often accommodate a home office and study area. Bedrooms, if large enough, are excellent since they offer privacy. Of course, the advantage of an entire room given over to a home office is that work can be left out, which is rarely the case when the office is only part of a room.

Regardless of location, all home offices need adequate storage space, good lighting, and enough electrical outlets to accommodate equipment such as a

© Robert Perron; Design: Charles Marks

typewriter, computer, telephone, and answering machine. The requirements vary depending on your tasks, equipment, and the type and quantity of papers and supplies you must store.

Specialized furniture is necessary in order to work comfortably at a computer or typewriter. Happily, the growth of home offices has produced a bumper crop of furniture geared to your needs. Since there's a trend toward homey colors, fabrics, and furniture in offices, you can select commercial pieces with

the special features you may have come to appreciate at work.

Channels that hold all those wires out of sight and untangled, electric outlets on the desk itself, correct heights for keyboards, file-storage drawers, generous work surfaces, and properly engineered office chairs are just as helpful at home as at the office.

The most comfortable height for typing at a typewriter or computer keyboard is 3 to 4 inches (7.5 to 10 cm) lower than standard desk height. If you find that it is impossible to provide a surface for this, you can compensate with an adjustable-height desk chair.

Good lighting is essential for desk work. While there are many choices of light source, including floor and table lamps and adjustable desk lamps, the important point is to have the light fall directly on the work and not the worker. Avoid glare by proper placement of the light.

◼ RIGHT:

The out-of-the-way location of this modular desk set makes sense in a city apartment where space is limited; also, the white-on-white color scheme makes it unobtrusive.

◼ FAR RIGHT:

If you can afford the space, a full study, with cabinets, shelves, and lots of natural light, is a great place to work.

Desks come in a variety of materials including natural and painted wood, plastic laminate, and metal. A well-lacquered wood surface, whether painted or natural, is advisable since it is easy to clean and can be wiped with a damp cloth and given added protection with a combination cleaning and polishing compound.

Laminates are also excellent, offering a tough, nonporous reasonably childproof surface that can probably defeat all but the most determined efforts at destruction. Laminates do not scratch easily. However, once scratched, they cannot be repaired.

When selecting a desk chair, opt for seating that is adjustable in several ways, especially if more than one person will be using the desk. Look for a chair that has an adjustable seat and back height, a tilting back, and a contoured seat and casters for added mobility.

The computer corner

Those who work with computers will likely find that furniture made for them (either custom-made or ready-made) works best. Before you go shopping for computer furniture, make sure you have mea-sured the dimensions of your equipment. Don't neglect to allow for the bulky wires and plugs at the rear of the components. When planning the printer's location, it may be necessary to allow space for continuous-feed paper to go into and out of the printer. Deal with the problem of printer noise by locating the telephone away from it (or by purchasing a quiet printer).

Choose low-glare surfaces because of the potential eyestrain that can develop after spending hours at the computer screen. Reflectance is a measure of how much light the surface is giving off. A heavily textured fabric has the least reflectance.

As a rule, the lighter the color the more reflectant it will be. Among the best color choices for computer areas are mauve and gray. However, you can choose almost any color by selecting it in a grayed hue. If your room happens to be quite dark, select lighter shades for walls, floors, and ceiling. If the opposite is true, opt for darker shades. In furniture it is a good idea to avoid high-gloss surfaces like those found in highly polished lacquered tables. If your computer screen is near a wall, don't select a bright, glaring print wall covering.

THE HOME GYM

Working out has become a popular at-home activity. How much space this hobby takes is totally dependent on how you pursue the laudable goal of physical fitness. Anyone can find enough space to jump rope in place for a half hour, and there are no storage requirements to speak of.

A greater investment of planning, money, and space is called for if your idea of fun extends to a stationary bike, a treadmill, an electronic stair machine, or even a ballet barre and full-length mirror.

Locations for a home gym include a spare bedroom, a corner of a family room, or a portion of a basement that can be reclaimed with new flooring and lighting. You could turn any closet into a storage spot for equipment, and the space immediately in front of it could serve as the workout area. If you opt for a corner of the bedroom, choose one in which it's possible to screen the equipment when not in use. Large bathrooms also are appropriate locations.

Most floors will easily accommodate a stationary bike and rowing machine, but if heavy machinery is part of your plan, check to make sure the floor will bear the weight. A local building inspector can probably suggest an engineer to give an informed opinion. The equipment manufacturer or retailer should provide specs on machinery weight and requirements. In an apartment house, the superintendent or building manager should be notified. You should also be certain the equipment you order will do the job you want and that you know how to operate it. The retailer can provide information on specific equipment and independent fitness experts can guide you on general equipment choices.

A satisfactory home exercise area should take as little upkeep as possible. Select a floor covering that wears well and requires little care. Both resilient vinyl with a no-wax finish and flat-weave carpeting are good choices. Make sure that there are no lifted edges that could cause someone to trip and avoid slippery floors that could lead to a fall.

If fabrics are required, absorbent materials such as terry cloth provide a comfortable surface on which to rest a sweaty body. Natural fabrics like cotton allow the body to "breathe" and are cool to the touch.

Open-weave holders such as baskets permit evaporation for exercise accessories such as wrist weights, jump ropes and barbells that get wet from perspiration. Vinyl coated wire bins hung on a closet door or the wall can hold bulky equipment, towels, and mats. Hooks and pegs mounted on the wall also work well and have the virtue of serving as functional decoration.

If you like to exercise to music or to a workout videotape, set up an audiovisual center with a television set, videocassette recorder, and storage for tapes. Putting mirrors on a wall or a portion of it helps you check technique and visually enlarges the space.

As for other wall decorations, posters or photos of athletes may spur you on to greater efforts. You can put color to work for you when selecting a color scheme. Cool colors such as pale blue and green provide a tranquil outdoorsy quality just right for an isometric exercise plan. Hot colors such as yellow and red can stimulate you, thus providing extra "energy" for aerobic dancing.

■

A spare bedroom is an ideal location for a home gym. Select a floor covering that wears well and requires little care, such as flat-weave carpeting.

H*Part Four*
HOME STYLES

Introduction

WHETHER YOU'RE DECORATING a large place or a small one, a sense of decorative unity throughout is desirable. In a small house, an atmosphere that is all of a piece is essential. Even in large houses, few people would feel comfortable in a setting that veers from great formality to rustic simplicity; where colors in one room clash with those of others; where a minimalist approach is taken in some rooms while others are heaped with accessories.

The variety available in furniture, accessories, fabrics, wallpaper, and finishes brings the world to your doorstep. Choose, however, to emphasize one or at most two styles and only a few related colors for a unified and comfortable home. This restriction is less limiting than you might think, since chances are that you, like most people, have strong style and color preferences.

A question to consider well before you get into a specific period or style is whether you prefer an informal or a formal environment. Differences between the relaxed way of life that's typical in a rural retreat and the more ordered lifestyle that's a feature of city life go beyond any particular time and place.

The distinction between rural comfort and city formality goes back to the classical period in Greece and Rome where different styles of furnishing characterized city residences and country villas. In succeeding eras, too, rural and urban styles each have had characteristic qualities, relating no doubt to the different kinds of activities pursued in each place.

In a city, the day's schedule is often closely planned, social occasions are arranged ahead of time, and life is usually compartmentalized into work, leisure, and rest. Breakfast at 7:30, leave for work at 8, home by 6, dinner, and so on. So many demands upon time, so much access to information, social and cultural activities, other people: All this calls for a fairly tight structure just to keep life on an even keel.

Befitting a structured way of life, city styles share certain characteristics, regardless of whether they date from the eighteenth, nineteenth or twentieth century. The furniture often has a glossy finish and

is made of exotic and costly woods such as mahogany and rosewood. You are meant to examine a piece closely so that you can appreciate details such as an inlaid pattern, a nice bit of carving, or an ornate trim. It's evident to the well informed that no expense has been spared to procure the best hardware, the most appropriate fabric, the most carefully matched veneers and fabrics.

Such niceties may seem excessive in a rural or suburban setting where activities are less structured and more relaxed. People are more likely to enjoy impromptu gatherings. Drop-in guests may be

■

City styles share certain characteristics, such as making open spaces appear larger than they really are.

If you are fortunate enough to have such an impressive staircase and balcony, take advantage of its unusual dimensions by using it to showcase a small sitting room.

■

If you are fortunate to have a view like this one, by all means take advantage of it.

invited to stay for a drink or a meal. The weather is more influential—a nice or a stormy day could lead to a change in plans.

Country cabinetmakers also improvise more. They may create an entire piece themselves, having no access to specialists. They may not be able to get the exotic materials so readily available in an urban center. So they substitute sturdy local materials, such as pine, for the unavailable teak or mahogany veneers.

Instead of paying top prices for precious hardware, shrewd country workmen may substitute a cruder copy of the fashionable accent. In this way, for example, wood knobs were used instead of brass in early American furniture. Country cabinetmakers dressed up wood pieces with paint, sometimes in imitation of the city fashions and sometimes as their own original contribution.

The scale of country furniture usually is bulkier than it is in city pieces. A country chest or chair may lack a certain refinement but make up for it in originality. The fabrics in a country room are usually of a rougher homespun material.

As styles of home decor, country and city are like well-cut tweeds or a dress suit. Both are attractive and you select the garment that suits your style and the occasion. Decorating has been emancipated! The modern sensibility accepts free rein in choice between informal and formal styles in city, suburb, and rural locations.

Most people probably create a home in the style they grew up with. If both styles appeal to you, however, and you find it difficult to make a choice, the location of your residence and the style of life you will be living offer guidelines. Making a strong and clear choice between a country and an urban style will produce the strongest room. It also will help you sort through the staggering number of decorative products available in the marketplace. The selection process is much more manageable when you can quickly eliminate items which are attractive but not appropriate to your plan.

If you don't know what style home you would like—which could indicate that you want a change

▪

The essence of country living: wicker baskets hung on wooden beams; cast-iron pots and pans; and all-wood cabinets and furniture.

from what you grew up with or that you've never given the matter any thought—begin your decorating project by familiarizing yourself with different styles and how they are being used these days.

Browse through recent decorating books and current magazines. Go window shopping in home furnishings stores. Attend decorative arts exhibitions at museums and galleries. Buy a ticket if there's a decorator showhouse open in your locality. Spring and fall are the usual seasons for these charity events in which designers decorate rooms of a mansion. All these sources offer a good introduction to the topic of style selection. You'll probably find there is a pattern to the rooms you favor.

©image/dennis krukowski; Design: Brenda Speight

Selecting a style

For a clue to your preferences between city and country styles, consider these questions:

▪ Do you like the idea of definite activities planned for each room?
▪ Do you prefer symmetrical arrangements of highly polished wood furniture and formal upholstery fabrics?
▪ Do you set a high value on tidiness?
▪ Does the calm of an all-white bedroom seem soothing?
▪ Do you enjoy a relaxed lifestyle in which you live in several undifferentiated spaces where you eat, sleep, and entertain, depending on mood and circumstances?
▪ Do you keep a month's worth of magazines handy and out in the open where you can grab one when you have a spare ten minutes?
▪ Does extra-large seating with soft edges and lots of cushions look best to your eye and feel most comfortable?
▪ Do starched white curtains and checked cotton fabrics seem like ideal choices for almost any room?

A yes to the first four questions marks you as a city-style person. A yes to the second four suggests you'd prefer informal country-style rooms.

COUNTRY STYLES

Many people prefer to live in homes that are traditional in feeling without specifically reflecting a single period or locale, homes that support an informal, comfortable way of life. If this is your preference, you will be happy in a country-style home. Comfort in both physical and aesthetic terms is the overall goal behind country style. Although a farm family might hold a different opinion, for most people the country exists as a place in which to retire to gain respite from the rules and rigors of city living.

Everything about a country place is more relaxed, including the mix of furniture and accessories. Old-fashioned pieces too dated or frayed for the city are refurbished and pressed into service. Meals often are taken in the kitchen instead of the dining room. Coats and hats are hung on a clothes tree in the hall instead of in a closet. Family pets have free rein. A

canary warbles away in a birdcage. Newspapers and magazines are stacked in the open.

In city living rooms, a television set or a home computer might be considered inappropriate. In a country living room, it's perfectly all right for the television to be out in full view. Displaying a computer, stereo components, books, and other paraphernalia reflecting personal interests does not offend, especially if they are neatly organized and unobtrusive.

Whether you're after American, Australian, English, or French country, or something more esoteric like Scandinavian or Greek country, you will find that simplicity in finishes and furnishings, rough textures, and bare floors (with rugs for comfort, not style) suit them all.

The special quality that distinguishes each and every country setting can be achieved with characteristic fabrics, a few items of furniture, and accessories. By varying the accents, you can produce a French manor house, an English Cotswold cottage, a country farmhouse, or whatever. In all country-style rooms there is likely to be considerable borrowing from many periods and places.

It's a great advantage in furnishing that reproductions from virtually all geographic areas are available. Copies of items that were found in many early farmhouses, like pie safes, painted chests, and Windsor chairs, have long been readily available at moderate prices. You will be able to find a copy of a French country armoire, an English chesterfield, or a rough-hewn oak or pine worktable. Recently, a vogue for painted Scandinavian pieces led several manufacturers to come out with reproductions, so these, too, can be found.

Often, it's the unique piece that ''makes'' the room, so shop also for authentic pieces in antiques stores and at auctions.

Since there are no special rules, country-style decorating is easier for a novice to execute than are period-style rooms. Another advantage is that the rooms are likely to look cheerful and attractive even in the disorder of family life. A scratch on a table doesn't ruin the effect.

AUSTRALIAN COUNTRY

Although Australian period decor has clear characteristics in wall, floor, and window treatments and furniture, decorating an Australian country room frees you from their strictures. You can easily include a mix of furnishings that were actually created over a hundred years.

Rather than trying to copy a room in a particular place or time, you may well prefer to pick and choose the elements that appeal to you. An attractive mix might include an antique or reproduction dresser containing a plate collection, Victorian wicker, and country pine chests. Pine, cedar, recycled timbers (such as oregon), and painted pieces can be used in the same room. For some floors you might choose rag rugs; for others, an oriental. Or perhaps you would like to strip back the floorboards to their natural state and polish them. Your walls could be painted plain white, stenciled, or wallpa-

■ *RIGHT:*
Instead of trying to recreate the design of a particular room, you may choose to mix and match a variety of styles.

■ *ABOVE, RIGHT:*
This rustic bedroom utilizes heavy wooden furniture to effect its western-style design.

© Phillip Ennis

pered and further ornamented with wallpaper borders to suggest or make up for architectural detailing that is lacking.

Rough fabrics of homespun cotton and linen and lively prints are equally appropriate, and simple country pottery is as suitable as flowered earthenware and hand-painted ceramic vases. Baskets of dried flowers or potted plants, folk paintings, art posters, or perhaps a still life in oils: It's up to you.

For a more contemporary feeling, choose clear colors and select accessories that are not too fussy. You can soften a room with antique linen and lace and floral fabrics. Tree trunk and branch furniture, rustic pine pieces, Australian hardwood and teak items, and old leadlight windows can all provide an edge to take the cuteness away from the style.

For ideas on how to carry out a particular theme, plan a trip to the area in which you're interested. Another source of ideas is movies. Rent a few costume dramas and study the settings that a movie professional has probably carefully researched. It can give you a visual impression of the style that will help you make the right decisions on fabrics, accessories, and room arrangements.

■ *BELOW:*
All the comforts of a country environment come together in this luscious porch setting, accenting the vibrant greens and reds.

■ *LEFT:*
A luxurious rustic lodge, adorned with patchwork quilts, large stone fireplace, and cast-iron collectibles.

Try westerns, for example, if you're after an American country look that incorporates motifs that were found in the American West. You'll soon observe that the western style tends to emphasize heavier furniture than was used in the Northeastern or Southern United States. It might be California Mission pieces, ornate but rough-hewn Spanish or Mexican furniture, or German-American Biedermeier pieces, which were taken out west by their owners who emigrated from the Midwest in the mid-nineteenth century—or all three. You'll probably find that colors from Indian blankets and the earthy hues of the soil, vegetation, and brilliant sunlit sky are excellent when it comes to selecting a color scheme.

AMERICAN RUSTIC

Rustic pieces made of recognizable parts of trees and the hides and horns of animals offer a characteristic country accent. Horn chairs, bearskin rugs, hat racks fashioned from antlers, and tables, chairs, and beds of tree branches, trunks, and twigs are all fascinating additions to a country room.

■ *The exposed wood on the ceiling of this room is perfect for the Southwestern Country look, further evoked here with the skull, cactus, and Indian-print throw pillows.*

The heyday for rustic furniture in the United States was between 1875 and 1925, says Craig Gilborn, author of *Adirondack Furniture and the Rustic Tradition*. Wealthy American families in this era built luxurious rustic lodges in areas such as the Adirondack Mountains and had them decorated and furnished by local artisans who used trees and hides, canvas and raffia. At its most primitive, the furniture was simple branches—bark and all— wedged or tied together and augmented with whatever other materials were handy to make utilitarian tables and chairs. Virtually every part of the tree was used for furniture—twigs, branches, trunk, burls, and roots.

Gilborn says that during the height of the fad for rustic pieces, parts of animals were a favorite material. He found records of orders for items like a thermometer made of porcupine feet and an inkwell from the hoof of a moose.

Actually, tree trunk and branch furniture substantially predates American rustic dwellings. The Chinese were using the materials for furniture several centuries before the Christian era. Still, it's a style associated with the American country ambience, and using a piece or two is a good way to create an interesting American country room.

The old pieces are rare and expensive. Look for reproductions, often at moderate prices, and new interpretations of rustic furniture and accessories.

ENGLISH COUNTRY

Versatile and comfortable, English country style has a great deal to offer someone who is seeking both distinctiveness and informality. There are both cottage and castle variants on the English country theme. So well-known is the former that you can probably close your eyes and easily conjure up a mental picture of a living room, even if you have never been to England.

You might imagine the room with overstuffed sofas and easy chairs covered in floral chintz that has faded with time. Whitewashed walls are embellished with a stenciled design around the windows where muslin curtains hang. A few portraits and landscape prints decorate the walls. The furniture consists of plain tables and chests with one or two fine-looking antique pieces—maybe a Welsh cupboard. There is at least one dog curled up in one of the chairs, a bouquet of dried flowers in an old marmalade jar or milk jug, and newspapers and magazines are casually piled on a table.

This picture makes it clear why the English country cottage has captured the world's imagination. A homier and cozier setting could hardly be imagined. The imaginary room seems to suggest the continuity of generations, all living in the same place. The family never threw anything out. When the finances could support it, additions and improvements were made. Perhaps a new bathroom or kitchen appliance would be installed or collapsing steps and a leaky roof would be replaced. When money wasn't to be had, the house and the family endured in shabbiness until the family fortunes revived.

■

The charm of this English Country room lies in its comfortable blend of lively decor and friendly informality.

Courtesy of Laura Ashley

■
This beautiful setting boasts floral patterns and a rich mix of accessories and art, displayed on the walls and tables.

Recreating the feeling of ancestral stability with occasional additions of the new is particularly apt if you're planning to furnish slowly on a limited budget.

A grander version of English country, as practiced primarily by famous decorators such as Keith Irvine, Sister Parish, and Mario Buatta, is altogether a more costly and demanding decorative style. It, too, is a mixture of antiques from a variety of periods and places, mementos and collectibles, all arranged for comfort and convenience.

Ironically, perhaps, an American woman played an important role in the development of the grand English country style as we know it today.

"Nancy Lancaster more than anyone in the world created the style that has come to be called country English decorating," says Keith Irvine, an English decorator who was one of the first to bring the look to the United States in the late 1950s.

Born in Virginia, she lived an upper-class life mainly in England where she was a well-known socialite and hostess and where she decorated several famous country houses. Though her houses were grand, Irvine says, "You could easily imagine a pair of dirty riding boots on the floor, and every room she had something to do with looked like a man had just left it."

Lancaster hired John Fowler to decorate her first English house, and then joined him in a business partnership at Colefax and Fowler. With what Irvine calls "her American know-how and Fowler's sense of color and knowledge of historic interiors and furnishings," they made the Colefax and Fowler style of English country a major influence in the world.

The American decorator Sister Parish was related to Nancy Lancaster, and when she came to England she fell under Fowler's influence, too, writes John Cornforth in his book, *The Inspiration of the Past.*

In 1958, Parish offered Irvine, who was Fowler's assistant, a job in New York. He soon set up his own shop and hired young Mario Buatta, who was just out of Parsons School of Design. Buatta made his own pilgrimage to England and to the sedate Colefax and Fowler showroom on Brook Street in London and the decorative glories of the English country house.

By the late 1960s, Buatta was creating his own affectionate versions of the English country look with chintz, ruffles, bows, and ribbon-festooned portraits of dogs.

The look, with its multiple floral patterns of chintz, elaborate fabric treatments for upholstery and window coverings, fine furniture of both English and European origin, and rich mix of accessories and art displayed on walls and tables, remains a durable style to the present. If it's for you, study the images of rooms found in many books and magazines and shop for reproductions or, if you can afford it, the real thing.

FRENCH COUNTRY

You don't need a decorating authority to tell you that a room with whitewashed walls, a terra-cotta tile floor, and a polished walnut armoire, or cupboard, is a French country–style room.

Those who have visited France's provinces know, however, that French country is an eclectic style with many different aspects. Depending on the building itself and grandness of the furniture, a French country room can be in a chateau or in a cottage. The characteristics these disparate rooms share include rough textures and bright sun-washed colors.

Instead of pale silk, you have the brightly patterned cotton fabrics of Provence. Instead of delicate crystal, there is a chunky hand-thrown pottery decorated perhaps with naive figures or flowers. Unpolished tile roofs, rush seats, carved dark wood cabinets, delicate painted pieces: All are of a rural character that places them far away from the smooth and sophisticated surfaces found in Paris.

A beautiful armoire can be the beginning of a French country room. French armoires are usually walnut or cherry and often feature carvings of flowers, wheat, or vine leaves. The armoire— perhaps as tall as 10 feet (3.2 m)—was often part of a bride's dowry and was passed down from one generation to the next. It had pride of place in the main room or master bedroom.

Today you can find lovely old and new armoires in the regulation wood finish or in paler bleached finishes with painted floral decoration. Though not authentic, the painted pieces are very attractive, especially in a warm climate. Today an armoire is more likely to hold home entertainment equipment, dinnerware, and barware than the linen that it may once have contained.

Courtesy of Tradition France

Courtesy of Tradition France

If you arrange the interior of an armoire attractively and line it with a Provençal cotton print, you may leave it open. Housewives in Provence lined their drawers, closets, and cupboards with Provençal fabrics and used the same fabric as curtains behind the bed and at the window and to make up cushions, tablecloths, napkins, and placemats.

In a French bedroom, a spectacular bed can be the focal point. A white mesh-draped metal bed with a canopy frame that comes to a center point is a romantic centerpiece in an adult's or child's bedroom. The sleigh bed or *bateau lit* is another standard in the French country bedroom. Sheets and pillowcases in white are traditional, embellished with family initials and perhaps some lace.

■ *ABOVE, LEFT:*
Often part of a bride's dowry, the traditional French Armoire was generally passed down from generation to generation.

■ *ABOVE:*
Armoires can be found in pale-bleached finishes with painted floral decoration.

Most country bedrooms were furnished simply with a minimum of possessions and accessories on display. Window treatments also were simple—lace panels are appropriate or curtains made of printed Provencal cotton or blue and white checks.

The quintessential French country fabrics are cotton and linen. Besides the vividly colored Provençal prints, plaids, jacquard fabrics, and printed *toile de Jouy* scenes can be used as upholstery, fabrics, and to cover walls.

A stucco-finish wall is ideal because it provides a rustic feeling. Terra-cotta tile, bare wood planking, and sisal, or sea grass, matting are all appropriate choices for floors. If you like the look of tile, but don't want to install it, try painting the floor with a *trompe l'oeil* tile pattern.

Dining chairs in French country rooms are rustic and simple. Rush seats are typical, but cane and ladderbacks are also used with rustic iron table bases with glass or marble tops or with plain rectangular wooden tables.

The upholstered easy chairs with exposed wood arms and legs, known as *bergeres*, in a formal home would be covered in velvet or damask. In a country room, they look great in bright plaids, stripes, or contemporary printed patterns.

Arrange furniture symmetrically and use pairs of furniture and accessories to create a strong feeling of balance. For example, place the same model of console table or chairs at either side of a door or sofa. Use a pair of candlesticks on a mantel.

Outfit a small kitchen with a round wooden tabletop on an iron base and several graceful iron-framed chairs. If it's a large country kitchen, look for a long scrubbed wooden table (an antique or recycled wood by preference).

There is nothing more typically French than the wicker or fruitwood bread holder known in France as a *panetière*. In France it would be hung in the kitchen and used to store bread and other foods.

Emphasize accessories such as pewter, glazed and unglazed ceramic pieces, copper pots, straw baskets, and dried flowers. For fresh flowers, favor potted geraniums and bunches of daisies.

■ *OPPOSITE PAGE:*
Vividly colored Provençal prints are used here as a tablecloth and wall coverings.

■ *LEFT:*
In a French bedroom, a spectacular bed can be the focal point, as this white metal bed with intricate detail indicates.

Study books and magazines to make a country-style kitchen uniquely your own. Borrow ideas from any era to design a comfortable setting.

Courtesy of Armstrong World Industries

CONTEMPORARY COUNTRY

Contemporary country may sound like a contradiction in terms, but it isn't: Country-style decorating is not tied to any actual historical period. The aim is to make a comfortable environment, borrowing freely from any era. The past is only one element in a stage setting that is shaped by you.

Some of the most interesting contemporary country rooms come from a vivid imagination fired by literary and travel associations. Think of the room you'd design for a hotel bedroom in Casablanca, a hill town of India, a Caribbean island, or an ancestral manor somewhere on the coast of Scotland.

It's quite possible that idea of home as a stage setting originated in department-store model rooms, which each season showcase the new furniture styles or are part of an overall store promotion of the crafts, apparel, and furnishings of exotic foreign countries like India, France, China, and Japan. Using the store decorator's tricks, you, too, can turn a room into a stage setting that is uniquely your own: a Swiss alpine cottage, a sheik's tent in a desert oasis, a penthouse in Miami. Study the coffee-table books and magazines that are part travelogue and part catalog. Filled with color photos, they are a good source of ideas for country-style decorating.

Let's say, for example, that you want to have a living room with a California country feeling. What images occur that you could use in the room? Many people might think of swimming pools, the blue Pacific, and palm trees. You might translate these thoughts into a blue-and-white color scheme and a mural that depicts palm trees.

"In Southern California, people have a tendency to live behind walls or gates in their own fantasy world," says California decorator Val Arnold. If you were to hire him to do "the Southern California look," he might suggest bleached floors, smooth plastered white walls, cotton dhurrie rugs, overstuffed white sofas, a round table and four large upholstered chairs on casters, a media center with an oversized television set and plenty of home-entertainment equipment, large, leafy tropical plants, and a few "stage prop" accessories such as a large wooden ball or a huge conch shell.

If California is calling, but you live elsewhere and aren't in the income bracket that imports its interior designers, here is Val Arnold's low-cost, do-it-yourself California living room done in several stages.

Step One: The walls are painted white; the floor is covered in sisal matting. Inexpensive mattresses are covered in a neutral or white sailcloth for seating. Bright-colored fabric is used to cover oversize throw cushions. A low Chinese coffee table and one lamp complete stage one.

Step Two: Install platforms to raise the mattresses off the floor. Add a large, green tropical plant, light, and a simple chair.

Step Three: Accessorize with a large oil painting, an artful accessory, and another table.

Step Four: The fourth stage—if you want it—is to add one or more antiques—Oriental first, European second.

Country-style furnishings

FURNITURE

Scrubbed pine, painted chests with simple lines, corner cabinets
Australian: Colonial furniture, iron bedstead, cedar dining table and chest
French: armoire, *panetière* (bread cupboard), rush-seated wood bench
English: Welsh dresser, Irish pine kitchen table, teakwood bench

FLOORS

Australian: polished floor boards, ceramic or quarry tiles, cork
French: terra-cotta or brick floor
English: stone floor, quarry tile, cork

WALLS

Plain white plaster or rough stucco walls, exposed ceiling beams, stucco finish walls, small-figured print wallpaper

FABRICS

Australian: striped and checked cottons, hand-painted and floral print fabrics
French: blue and white, *toile de Jouy*, Souleiado prints from Provence in yellow, orange, and red, paisley print
English: Laura Ashley prints, sprigged muslin, wide awning stripes

WINDOWS

Lace curtains, shutters, bamboo blinds, simple cotton curtains with gathered top

ACCESSORIES

Copper pots, houseplants in terra-cotta pots, rough pottery urns, birdcages, dried flowers and wreaths, heavy white ceramic ware, stoneware vases and bowls, salt-glaze crocks, pictorial tiles

■ *A simple floral arrangement and table decorate the entryway to this home.*

PERIOD STYLES

■

This colorful bathroom combines a late-nineteenth-century Victorian touch with an early-twentieth-century Art Deco design.

copy virtually any style. Not only furniture, but wall coverings, floor coverings, and accessories are widely available to re-create the look you like.

Some popular examples of early-nineteenth-century period style include England's Queen Anne, Georgian, and Regency periods. The most popular mid- to late-nineteenth-century style is Victorianism in all its varieties. Early-twentieth-century period styles include Art Deco, Arts and Crafts, and early Bauhaus modern. Just remember that any particular period style will have its drawbacks—don't authenticate at comfort's expense.

MAKING PERIOD DECOR LIVABLE

In home decorating, the wish to return to the distant past is difficult to put into practice. It's impossible to live a late-twentieth-century life with eighteenth- or even nineteenth-century furnishings. Modern bathrooms and kitchens as well as television sets and stereos are only a few of the things that most people would prefer to have, despite their allegiance to period decor. Since homes are for living, the thought of total authenticity has been abandoned in favor of a more realistic attitude. Even dedicated preservationists are likely to agree that a love for the past does not require people to live without modern conveniences.

Few decorators would hesitate to employ comfortable upholstery in an eighteenth-century room, especially since there really is no period upholstery that meets contemporary ideas of comfort. In the dining room, an extension table of modern origin is often a necessity, and in a bedroom or family room that lacks closets, installing a modern wall system may be the only solution.

It's clear that in the past, just as today, styles changed frequently. Upholstery fabrics, window treatments, wallpaper, and paint styles were especially subject to change. Floors also were covered differently depending on tastes and finances. Polished wood with fine Orientals, rag rugs, and carpeting were all used in houses of the same period and locale.

While it is time-consuming and usually expensive to decorate a period home in appropriate detail, the effort can be rewarding in terms of psychic comfort. Not only does a period room recall a familiar and well-loved part of the past, it's often the best choice for a residence with period architecture.

Interiors that are true in most of their details to the specific historical period of the building in which they are situated have an almost indefinable "right" feeling. The authentic room contributes to a feeling of emotional comfort.

With reproduction furnishings widely available these days, you can find the ingredients needed to

On the other hand, doors, windows, and fireplaces were less likely to undergo significant alteration. These elements are so much a part of the architecture that it's often worth the effort to retain or restore them as constructed when redoing an old house.

As you plan the remodeling of a room or home, learn the approximate date and style of the period that you are duplicating. Then find authentic examples of homes of the period, both in actuality and in pictures. Consult books on period interiors. Historic house museums and reconstructed villages are treasure troves of information. The United States is particularly rich in historic house museums. Other countries—such as England, France, and Denmark—also offer rich pickings in museums dedicated to the decorative arts. Their curators and publications are good resources for ideas.

■

This regal bedroom is adorned with a fine canopy bed and judiciously placed antiques.

To furnish period rooms economically, use reproductions with a few judiciously placed antiques. An executive at an American fabric firm estimated that approximately 75 percent of the company's print fabrics are either exact reproductions or adaptations of traditional styles. These are available in both the authentic color (known as the documentary color) and in colorations geared to the present. Home-furnishings manufacturers generally treat antique styles as their resource material. Consequently, finding what you need may simply require familiarity with the historic style you are replicating.

Once, those who could afford them invariably chose antiques over reproductions. Nowadays, when the best original designs are often in a museum, too expensive, the wrong dimension, or too fragile, the reproduction can be the better choice. This change in thinking is also a tribute to improvements in the copies. Many are more accurate, so they don't stick out like a sore thumb when mixed with antiques.

An important appeal of exact copies is their historic associations. It's helpful to know the terms *replica, reproduction,* and *adaptation* before you go shopping. The first two are generally used interchangeably, but *replica* carries the strongest identification with an original. It is a line-for-line copy of an existing piece of furniture. As far as possible, the same materials and methods of construction are employed as in the original.

A *reproduction* is also a line-for-line copy of an original piece, which is identified by name. In some instances, liberties may have been taken in construction, finish, or type of wood. Both replicas and reproductions are usually stamped or marked in some way to identify them.

An *adaptation* is based on the kind of furniture it emulates. It may be very true to the original, differing only in dimensions, or it may be quite fanciful.

Expect to pay a premium for a replica of a museum original. First of all, they usually cost more to make than similar new period pieces. Second, the cooperating museum earns a royalty on each piece sold. Advertising costs may be higher since glossy promotional materials are usually prepared to promote the collection.

Reproductions, if kept in good condition, can appreciate in value over the years. However, especially with nineteenth-century pieces, which are still fairly common, sometimes you can own the antique for about the same price as the reproduction. So it is wise to comparison-shop in antiques stores and auctions when buying furniture. For an accurate comparison, figure in the cost of restoration, which may be required to put the old piece in shape for use.

RENOVATING AN OLD HOUSE

The desire to reflect accurately how period rooms really looked has never been greater, despite the wish for modern conveniences. There are three schools of thought to the addition of modern features: Hide them, flaunt them, or zone them. The first method places modern necessities such as computers and televisions behind closed doors. The

■

A four-poster canopy bed is highlighted with a patchwork quilt and white lace pillows.

Courtesy of Brooks Roge's Inc.

second has no problem with an Amish quilt, a rocking chair, and a computer in the same room.

The third approach divides the house up into period and modern areas. The parlor or lounge may be in character with the period of the house, and the kitchen high tech. Of course, sometimes all three solutions are employed in the same house, but the idea of zoning a house is perhaps the most accepted stratagem nowadays.

Many people prefer to keep features once routinely eliminated in the interest of modernization. They tend to find odd spaces like broom closets and pantries appealing and are willing to undertake the added expense of building on to a house at the rear so that the original building can be left as is.

A wing added to the back can accommodate a new kitchen and family room. Upstairs, the new space would accommodate a master bedroom and bath.

Being sympathetic to a structure sometimes means putting back detail removed by earlier occupants. Perhaps the shutters of a Colonial were taken off or painted the same color as the rest of the house in an earlier attempt at modernization. If you were to repaint them in a different color, you could

■ *LEFT*:
This sitting room has a unique Victorian rustic charm.

give the house back some of its dignity. Painting the front door a different color from the rest of the front also works wonders.

Other decorative exterior projects that can make a difference include the addition of a brass knocker and an appropriate period lighting fixture. At greater cost, you might add on a vestibule or entryway, a front or back porch, or a covered breezeway. Sometimes new landscaping alone is all that's needed. Just cleaning a stone foundation that has been mistakenly painted so it shows is like putting a house on a pedestal.

It is typical for a Victorian to be missing some of its architectural trim. Interesting details may still be there but go unnoticed because of the single-color paint job that has replaced an original multicolor exterior that highlighted the details. A new paint job for the trim may do the trick.

■ *FAR LEFT*:
Antique bric-a-brac abounds in this lovely slanted-roof bedroom.

■
The combination of Japanese, English regency, and French pieces adds to an invigorating decor. These days, decorating rules can be broken as long as you retain a unified feeling among the furnishings.

Mixing styles

These days, few decorating rules are regarded as inviolate. However, keeping a similar feeling in the furnishings you select is safest for novices. So if you're furnishing a formal Victorian room and need more storage, remember that freestanding storage pieces are more in character with that style than a wall system would be.

Sometimes, however, adding an element from a different period invigorates decor. The lines of the pieces dictate how well they marry. You could combine a seventeenth-century Italian table and chairs with contemporary furniture and lamps because their lines complement one another. Mixing furniture and accessories from different periods is a trial-and-error process.

Experience suggests that contemporary lacquered cabinetry goes well with oriental and Art Deco accessories. Pleated shades or Shoji screens at the windows and Regency chairs would not be out of place in such a room. You can safely combine Japanese, Shaker, and Scandinavian modern furniture. English Regency and Chinese furniture work together. The rounded forms of eighteenth-century French pieces, Art Nouveau, and Victorian also marry well. All are sophisticated city styles and share a certain formality.

NEOCLASSICISM

Periodically, the architecture and art of ancient Egypt or the classical civilizations of Greece and Rome are reinterpreted in home decorating for a new age.

Each era discovers for itself the aesthetic pleasures of the classical rules of proportion that were worked out in Grecian temples. Decorative motifs such as the acanthus leaf, the laurel wreath, and the acorn are revived. Materials such as stone and terra-cotta, frescoed walls, and the orange-hued and black color scheme of Greek vases once again look fresh.

Recalling classical designs started in the Renaissance when, after a long period of loss, the glories of ancient Greece and Rome were rediscovered by scholars and artists. Excavations at Pompeii and Herculaneum during the eighteenth century uncovered buried homes of the classical age. For the first time, there was reliable information on how those homes had been furnished. These archaeological discoveries created a Neoclassical fashion that was interpreted slightly differently in various countries and by diverse individuals.

Architects and designers began to ornament buildings and furniture with classical motifs such as pilasters and cornices. New shapes for chairs, such as the Grecian-derived, X-shaped *klismos*, were developed. The art of fresco was practiced on walls and panels. Plaster busts were placed on pedestals, and the faded pink of aged terra-cotta and gray of stone once again were used.

Since the eighteenth century, Neoclassical design themes have regularly been revived in virtually every western country. In the United States, the Federal period of the late-eighteenth and early-nineteenth centuries is the main Neoclassical furniture design period. In architecture, the Greek Revival style of the mid-nineteenth century is Neoclassical.

In England, Palladian, Empire, and Regency are Neoclassical styles. In France, the Directoire and Empire periods of the nineteenth century are Neoclassical. The design influence known as Biedermeier, which reached its height between 1815 and 1850, characterizes the preeminent Neoclassical design influence in northern Europe, especially Austria, Germany, and Scandinavia.

All the Neoclassical styles emphasize austere furniture lines relieved by Neoclassical ornamentation, military and Egyptian motifs on fabric and wall coverings, asymmetrical window coverings often of sheer fabrics. Colors are light, but contrasts between blond wood and ebony insets, for example, are dramatic.

Since classical architecture is based on restraint and on specific rules of scale, balance, and proportion, it is outside the standard definition of old or new. The style can be used to create both traditional and modern rooms.

© Phillip Ennis

■ *ABOVE:*
The architecture of the classic civilizations of Greece and Rome are reinterpreted in home decorating for a new age.

■ *OPPOSITE PAGE:*
Asymmetrical window coverings of sheer fabrics and replicas of ancient Greek furniture accent this Egyptian-influenced living room.

During the twentieth century, Neoclassical revivals have frequently occurred. They include some aspects of Art Deco and Postmodernism and a new vogue for Biedermeier furniture. Some theorists assert that the Neoclassical influence will be one of the strongest traditional design influences in the 1990s. This versatile design theme produces a room that is quiet without being bland. Neoclassical styles are particularly useful when you want to accentuate a room's architectural distinction. But rooms devoid of interest can be made more appealing with the addition of Neoclassical furnishings and ornamentation. The style also imparts warmth to contemporary rooms.

Though each version has its own particulars, they share inspirations, so Neoclassical styles can be mixed with one another. "You can use English or French Regency furniture or even Louis XIV, Art Deco, or Biedermeier pieces and Bauhaus modern," says New York–based designer Jay Spectre whose preferred "moderne" style of decorating owes much to Neoclassicism.

Spectre's description of moderne shows how one designer mixes periods to create a Neoclassical effect. Imagine an urbane Hollywood movie set from the 1930s with its black or white lacquer furniture, Art Deco figurines, classical busts, Venetian glass mirrors, obelisks, and Egyptian-inspired objects.

Spectre would update it with metallic accents such as moldings or baseboards painted silver or gold. A modern room in the neoclassic theme he orchestrated has dark green walls with gold stenciled astrological design, beige upholstery, and black accents. A characteristic modern color scheme combines black furniture, ivory walls, and touches of Chinese red. Country floral print fabrics and wallpaper would be inappropriate in a Neoclassical room, but you can have flowers if you choose a stylized Deco floral print.

A choice floor treatment is wall-to-wall carpet in a velvet plush. An octagonal, hexagonal, or round area rug on a highly polished wood floor or a diamond pattern in black and white are also appropriate choices.

Neoclassic decoration

FURNITURE

Chaise, reproduction or interpretation of Greek *klismos* chair, straight-lined sofa, light pieces with slender legs, Biedermeier cabinet with drop-leaf desk, light woods in honey-brown and gold tones with ebony inlays, reproduction Sheraton and Duncan Phyfe furniture, Hitchcock chair with painted historic scene on chair back

FLOORS

Parquet with geometric or diamond patterns, marble or tile, smooth plush carpet in white, beige, gray

WALLS

Stenciled designs or wallpaper borders with laurel wreath, Greek key, lyre, acanthus leaf motifs; *trompe l'oeil* scene, faux marble baseboards, statues in niches

FABRICS

Plain woolens, vibrant-colored silk, tented ceilings, stylized floral wallpaper

WINDOWS

Pleated white muslin curtains, silk drapes in bright green, yellow, and crimson, asymmetrical arrangements of sheer fabrics on windows

ACCESSORIES

Elaborate clock under glass dome, porcelain bust, round gilt-framed mirror, Grecian urns in red and black, Egyptian statues

A large oriental rug and Chesterfield sofa are just a few of the luxurious examples of stunning Victorian design in The Mansion, an inn in Rock City Falls, NY.

VICTORIAN DESIGN

Queen Victoria graced the British throne from 1837 to 1900. During her reign, when England was the world's richest country, attending to British economic interests sent Englishmen to exotic India, Africa, the Middle and Far East, even as far as the steppes of Russia. Scientific discoveries, mass production and mass education also increased in the British Empire, the United States, and Europe.

The decorative consequence of these economic and social developments was Victorianism: an eclectic set of styles that rapidly succeeded one another as architects and designers plundered the past as well as other cultures in order to decorate the homes of the newly wealthy middle classes.

Queen Victoria, an enthusiastic amateur decorator when young, is said to have appreciated light woods, clear, light blue and green, and large win-

dows so that natural light could suffuse a room. However, as time went on, the tenor of Victorian design turned. The exuberant Victorians rarely left well enough alone, and Victorianism became a style of excess rather than restraint. Ornate carved furniture, patterned wall and floor coverings, layered window treatments with extensive fabric trimmings, antiques, stuffed animals, knickknacks, framed photos, music boxes, and pianos draped with paisley shawls were thrown together with reckless abandon.

Furniture was copied or adapted from models from the French and Italian Renaissance, Baroque, Gothic, and Rococo periods. Often several styles were used in the same house. In her book *Period Details*, Mary Gilliatt says that the lighter and more feminine eighteenth-century French styles were considered suitable for ladies' boudoirs and party rooms. Renaissance styles were thought more appropriate for rooms such as libraries and dining rooms.

The grand Victorian house, with its separate entry hall, drawing room, morning room (a kind of informal living room equivalent perhaps to today's family room), and formal dining room, was well suited to the heavy and elaborate pieces with which it was furnished. The amalgam of architecture, interior design, and attitude is what's being celebrated in today's revival of Victorian design.

"We had to go back to the Victorians in order to find a model for our own retreat into cocooning," says Katherine C. Grier, author of *Culture and Comfort: People, Parlors and Upholstery, 1850–1930.*

The Victorians covered almost every square inch of their rooms with fabric, including fireplace mantels and shelves. While the coffee table didn't exist, a tea table was part of the Victorian parlor. Every parlor had a center table, which usually was covered with a cloth and held a prized family possession such as a bible or photo album as well as a lamp. Quite a few households had a piano or, by the 1870s, a parlor organ, which was less expensive.

While telephones appeared in 1880s in urban places, they were not common until well into the twentieth century, and they would have been in a hallway, not a parlor. Ashtrays would not have been in a parlor since polite people didn't smoke there.

As she researched the past, Grier discovered that most of the mechanisms used today to inform consumers about decorating fell into place during the course of the nineteenth century.

"Of course, there was no radio or television but there were women's magazines and decorating publications, especially by the 1870s. People also took their cues from parlors in commercial establishments and hotels. By the 1890s the model room in a furniture store was a huge selling point," said Grier. The Graves Furniture Store in Rochester, New

▪ *OPPOSITE PAGE:*
The essence of Victorian design lies in its adherence to lavish variety; although the look is coherent, the overall impression is one of entropy.

▪ *BELOW:*
A variety of textures and patterns unite to give this dining room a comfortable and sprightly appearance.

York, for example, advertised that it had on display a furnished, eight-room model house as well as a more modest five-room flat.

"Consumer credit for furniture was in place by the 1880s, so people could buy whole rooms on the installment plan. By the mid-nineteenth century, makers were building furniture on speculation, but the decade for the development of inexpensive attractive mass-produced furniture was the 1870s," she said. During the 1890s, there was an even greater proliferation of factories making inexpensive furniture for the middle and lower middle classes.

Prices varied widely depending on the amount of care taken and cost of materials. A divan with an adjustable arm might have cost between $6 and $10. Even though mass-produced furnishings were available, homemakers were encouraged to exercise personal taste and to embrace do-it-yourselfism.

The art needlework craze of the 1880s had women embroidering and painting on fabric, and appliqué and macrame were popular. Americans made over old ladderback chairs into upholstered easy chairs well into the twentieth century. In magazines of the period, many articles told how to fashion homemade upholstered furniture by recycling other materials. There were directions for constructing sofa and chair frames of hardwood and also for reupholstering secondhand furniture. How to make lambrequins, which are flat valances, for mantels, tablecloths, window, and door drapery and cut down draperies and bedspreads to make curtains were also popular subjects.

The January 1859 issue of Godey's *Lady's Book* instructed readers how to make upholstered furniture from packing boxes, barrels, and fabric. The article advised sawing out parts of a flour barrel, installing webbing and then laying on this structure a layer of coarse bagging, stuffing it with bran, and covering it all with chintz-covered cushions.

Although by the end of the nineteenth century mass-produced fabric furnishings and furniture made such economies unnecessary for much of the middle class, authors of domestic economy and decorating advice books were still emphasizing do-it-yourself projects as a thrifty way to obtain attractive furnishings.

Such similarities in attitude and interests perhaps make it easy for us in the 1990s to duplicate and appreciate the homes of the 1890s.

Other late-nineteenth-century styles

Not every late-nineteenth-century interior was furnished in fussy high Victorian style. Some people, especially those with advanced tastes, preferred a less cluttered interior. Besides Neoclassical styles, which continued especially in Scandinavia, an interest in craftsmanship quietly grew.

In rural parts of the United States, for example, local craftsmen turned out simple chests, chairs, and tables. Working apart from the mainstream, the Shakers made simple, spare furniture for themselves and to sell. In 1876 a celebration of America's one-hundredth birthday in Philadelphia included several exhibits devoted to American Colonial life and stimulated a revival of American Colonial style furniture.

The Philadelphia Centennial also celebrated the movement known as Aestheticism. The goal of the Aesthetic movement was to glorify craftsmanship and artistry in the design of buildings and home furnishings. Devotees of Aestheticism also venerated newly discovered Japanese fabrics and wallpaper and ceramic wares. This enthusiasm for Japanese style led to Art Nouveau, which has been called the first twentieth-century style.

The Aesthetic principles of simplicity, craftsmanship, and a unified relationship between building and decor and interior and exterior were the seeds that helped to spur the growth of twentieth-century Modernism.

Victorian-style furnishings

FURNITURE

Chesterfield, Belter-style furniture, marble-topped table, leather easy chair with button tufting, mirrored mahogany hat stand, hall tree, whatnot, circular dining table with pedestal base

FLOORS

Floral-pattern rug, several small orientals used in the same room

WALLS

Ornate wallpaper in botanical patterns and imitating damask, satin, and brocade fabrics, painted picture rail, dark painted woodwork, patterned tin ceiling, walls covered with paintings

FABRICS

Needlepoint cord and fringe-trimmed damask and silk, cut velvet, plain velvet in deep colors, tartan plaid

WINDOWS

Stained-glass windows, large-paned windows, elaborate window treatments with double curtains, undercurtains of lace, overdrapes of heavy fabrics trimmed with cord that puddle on floor, tiebacks hung low

ACCESSORIES

Porcelain busts, pedestals for plants or sculpture, art pottery, tables covered with framed photographs and odds and ends, lace tablecloths and doilies, needlework cushions

Chapter 3

Modern Styles

Modern is a decorative style with variations enough to satisfy both a traditionalist and an iconoclast. The twentieth century has produced almost one hundred years of innovations—more if you admit into the pantheon the Art Nouveau and the Arts and Crafts movements, which straddle the nineteenth and twentieth centuries, and Art Deco. All three of these design themes recently have been reevaluated and revived.

Furnishing in modern style can satisfy those who enjoy being in a vanguard, who wish to recall their own personal journey through time, who require a functional interior and who want to stretch limited funds.

In this chapter we look at the development of modern styles, attempting to clear up some of the inevitable confusion that results from calling so many different decorative approaches by the same name.

Victorianism held sway as the twentieth century opened, but the Art Nouveau and Arts and Crafts movements, which were the modernism of their time, were sowing seeds of change that eventually would culminate in full-fledged Modernism.

■ *ABOVE:*
Modernism stripped furniture of its heavy, Victorian ornamentation.

■ *BELOW, RIGHT:*
Furniture in the Arts and Crafts style highlighted building skills and fine materials; it also recalled the designs of previous eras.

■ *FAR RIGHT:*
The Arts and Crafts movement, formed in response to the aesthetically excessive Victorian style, emphasized a down-to-earth accessibility; it focused on practicality and the recognition of skilled craftsmanship.

ARTS AND CRAFTS

Born in the nineteenth century, arts and crafts perhaps reached its greatest popularity in the early part of the twentieth century. Its fundamental premise was that the mass-produced decorative furnishings of the Victorian era were debased with fake ornamentation and that their use devalued honest labor and fine workmanship.

The way around a morally and aesthetically bankrupt Victorianism was to revert to hand craftsmanship, which had flowered earlier, for example, during the late medieval period of craftmen's guilds.

Late nineteenth-century craftsmen-theorists such as William Morris in England and Gustav Stickley in the United States aimed to produce designs inspired by the values of truth to materials and fitness for purpose. The actual designs to accomplish the purpose varied from country to country and over several decades. Plain oak furniture of straight, square lines with visible joinery could look as if it originated in the middle ages or as if it were put together in a rural workshop.

■ *LEFT:*
This room is typical of modern design; notice the sleek lines of the furniture and accessories, and the sharp contrast between black and white in the color scheme.

Morris, for example, was inspired by medieval motifs in his fabrics and wall coverings and interior design schemes. Stickley's furniture and accessories were more in the country motif. Many craftsmen based designs on forms that they contrived from the world of nature.

Today, the original simple rectilinear furniture and unmistakable lamps, silver, ceramic tiles, and domestic articles are greatly appreciated, and therefore are costly and collectible. Reproducing the look has become both popular and possible since copies of the originals are being made.

Architectural elements to consider for rooms in the Arts and Crafts style are polished or painted wood paneling, stained-glass windows, built-in window seats, and polished parquet wood or tile floors. A decorative idea that is peculiarly associated with the period is stenciled mottos (a Biblical quotation, for example) on the wall around the fireplace or near the ceiling.

ART NOUVEAU

The turn-of-the-century style known best by its French nomenclature spanned geographic borders in Europe and the United States and was called by other names as well, such as *Jugendstil* in Germany, the Viennese Secession in Austria, and the *Stile Liberty* or *Floreale* in Italy.

Art Nouveau (literally translated meaning new art) is firmly linked with the 1890s. The style lasted about a decade, but in its lack of ties to any specific historical predecessor it's an important antecedent of Modernism, which also was characterized by a lack of historic connection.

Though there were national differences, a common feature of all the styles was their extravagant floralism. "Sinuously weaving forms that resemble plants moving underwater," is the description given by design historian Charles McCorquodale. Other commonalities were the use of forms and colors found in Japanese art, silken textiles, floral- and fruit-derived colors, and a fascination with the female form.

© Cooper Hewitt Museum

■ *OPPOSITE PAGE:*
This clock is typical of the Arts and Crafts style; the rich wood paneling of its casing and its simple, rectangular shape emphasize the care that went into its construction.

■ *ABOVE:*
Tiffany lamps were fashionable accessories during the spread of Art Nouveau.

The graceful arabesques of iron that Hector Guimard fashioned into signs for Metro stops in Paris are among the most famous surviving examples of Art Nouveau. The internationalism of the style is clearly demonstrated, however, in the mixed nationalities of its most famous practitioners, which includes designers from Spain to Scotland.

The Belgian Victor Horta is usually credited with being the first to create Art Nouveau residences in which tendril-like iron stair railings and architectural decorations are characteristic. Scotsman Charles Rennie Mackintosh, Spaniard Antoni Gaudi and American Louis Comfort Tiffany also are associated with Art Nouveau.

Mackintosh's elongated Egyptian-like female figures and luscious color combinations such as lilac, pink, tender green, and white were particularly arresting. He coordinated every element in his schemes, even the flower arrangements. His inventive elongated furniture designs contain elements of Arts and Crafts ideas.

Gaudi's remarkable buildings, erected mainly in and around Barcelona, look like the drip castles made with wet sand by children playing on the beach. Several of his apartment houses have no right angles.

The spread of Art Nouveau in the United States was fostered by Louis Comfort Tiffany, whose stained-glass windows and lamps and iridescent Favrile glass were all immensely fashionable and greatly admired.

Few people wish to reproduce the style in its entirety today. However, a touch of Art Nouveau can add a lively, artful, and appealing accent to any room in your home. If you choose to partake of the style, choose wallpaper and fabrics with curving motifs of branches, flowers, leaves, and stems. Color schemes emphasize light colors such as white, gray-green, lilac, salmon pink. Employ some black to lend crispness. Appropriate accessories are a Tiffany-style table or floor lamp, a Japanese umbrella, a bamboo table or cabinet, a curved wrought-iron stair rail and grille work on windows, doors, or furniture.

AMERICAN PRAIRIE STYLE

During a seventy-year career, Frank Lloyd Wright, arguably America's greatest modern architect, designed 430 homes of which 360 have survived. During his exceptionally long and productive career, Wright changed his approach somewhat from the early Prairie style that is allied with the Arts and Crafts movement to a modernism that is at home in the later part of the twentieth century.

He revealed a love for and knowledge of Oriental (especially Japanese) art in details that share some characteristics with Art Nouveau. But all of his work has a warmth that appeals to many people who find other examples of Modernism cold.

Elements of his designs that seem especially relevant today include extensive use of wood with special attention to beautiful graining in woods such as natural oak, closely tying furnishings to architecture, fitting building to landscape, and locating windows to take advantage of views. A feeling of repose is evident in most of the residences he designed.

His concern for those of modest means makes Wright rather rare among famous architects. His Usonian-style homes, for example, were supposed to be affordable by the average middle-income American. These buildings shared the distinctiveness of his more luxurious projects. He pioneered such cost-cutting features as heated concrete floors, a geometric grid for easy construction, rooms opening into each other without the usual halls and doors, and built-in plywood furniture.

Despite the fact that Wright has been dead since 1959, the number of houses and products reproduced grows rather than diminishes with the years. Furthermore, original furnishings by Wright now are recognized and expensive collectibles.

Using reproductions of his designs, those who appreciate his masterly touch can create their own Frank Lloyd Wright interior. Furniture, fabric, rugs, stained-glass windows, silver, dishes, and lamps are available in reproductions and adaptations.

To experience an actual Wright interior, you can visit restored houses by the architect in a number of places in the United States, including Oak Park and Chicago, Illinois, Buffalo, New York, Hollywood, California, and Wright's own studios and houses in Spring Green, Wisconsin and Tucson, Arizona.

■ *ABOVE AND RIGHT:*
The use of clean, rectilinear design and the emphasis on the grain of fine woods characterize Frank Lloyd Wright's unique synthesis of decorative elements from both early Prairie style and Japanese art.

ART DECO

More an attitude that embraced innovations in materials, art, music, and fashion that occurred between the two world wars than a single specific decorative style, Art Deco shared the decades of the 1920s and 1930s with early Modernism. France provided the name in a shorthand reference to a seminal exhibition in Paris in 1925: the Exposition Internationale des Arts Décoratifs et Industriels Modernes.

Unlike Modernism, which focused exclusively on the new, Art Deco incorporated aspects of the past in Neoclassicism, as noted in the prior chapter, Rococo furniture, Orientalism, and primitive art. It drew, too, on novel entertainments such as jazz, the tango, and modern ballet, on a fad for Egyptian decoration, the art of Cubism, and streamlining, a representation of the aerodynamic lines of trains, steamships, and automobiles, as well as the use of the new materials, such as plastic.

■

A functional approach to living called for eliminating the unnecessary.

■*ABOVE AND ABOVE, TOP: Art Deco design focused on the use of materials that were new (like plastic) and shapes that were streamlined; these two serving trays are good examples of the slick shapes and dramatic color schemes that characterized the Art Deco style.*

The most exquisite examples of Art Deco—furniture by Jacques-Emile Ruhlmann, Jean Dunand, and Jean Michel Frank, for example—were always costly, exotic, and rare. However, one could also buy inexpensive, mass-produced furniture and crass metal, plastic and ceramic objects.

Since Art Deco covered such a wide range, there's a great deal of latitude in styling an Art Deco room. Other than motifs already mentioned, some design elements that lend the right character include streamlined furniture in exotic woods and lacquer finishes; walls, floors, and ornaments with stylized geometric designs; shiny materials such as mirror and chrome; silver and gold metallic finishes for decorative objects; Egyptian-looking art objects; and fabrics with stylized jazz age figures. Dramatic contrasting color schemes (mauve, gold, and black, or pink, brown, and black, for example) are characteristic.

MODERNISM

The style that came to dominate twentieth-century design rejected revivals in favor of a new departure. As Edgar Kaufmann, Jr., wrote in a Museum of Modern Art publication in 1950: "Designs made now in mimicry of past periods or remote ways of life ('authentic Chippendale reproductions' or 'Chinese modern') cannot be considered as anything more than embarrassing indications of a lack of faith in our own values."

Furthermore, whereas other styles could be identified by specific types of surface ornament and pattern, modernism rejected applied ornament in favor of what was known as pure form. A functional approach to living eliminated whatever was considered unnecessary. So carving came off furniture, pattern was eliminated from walls and fabric surfaces, and tables were cleared of objects.

Moldings, paneling, bric-à-brac, framed photographs, and doilies were banished. Lighting was ideally provided by fixtures instead of table lamps. In place of undisciplined individual furniture items in idiosyncratic shapes, wall systems and modular seating were introduced.

Some of the most influential reformers were architects, designers, and artists who worked and taught at the Bauhaus, a design school founded by Walter Gropius in Germany in the early part of the twentieth century. The school operated from 1919 to 1933 until Naziism forced its close. However, its leaders emigrated mostly to the United States, where they had even more influence.

An overall aim of the Bauhaus was to offer the fruits of rational design to everyone in the form of

© Derrick & Love/room design by Andre Putman

■ *FAR LEFT:*
Following the tenets of Modernism, lighting is ideally accomplished by fixtures instead of lamps, and pure, streamlined forms are applied.

■ *LEFT:*
Energetic angles and stimulating color patterns are typical in a warm and playful Modern environment.

inexpensive furnishings. This visionary goal was not really achieved. But the design philosophy of the Bauhaus and the International Style that followed it and shared the same values did succeed in becoming the mainstream modern style.

Though rather austere in its purest form, it continues to serve those who employ it with functional and beautiful interiors. Many people believe that the International Style will rank with earlier great architectural and decorative contributions.

■ *LEFT:*
Rationing of accessories and restriction of surface pattern and ornament can make a room seem severe, but can also be refreshing and inspirational.

Modern rooms have been characterized as colorful and devoid of color, machine-made and hand-crafted, understated and flamboyant, society's savior and its destroyer. These contradictions alone would warn someone that creating a modern room is not without its hazards.

To duplicate the style, it's important to understand it in depth. Straight-edged rectilinear furniture, rationing of accessories, and restriction of surface pattern and ornament can make for a severe environment. But modern can be warm, playful, and visually stimulating, particularly when streamlined and naturally rounded or biomorphic forms, graceful arcs, and energetic angles are added to the design vocabulary.

Streamlining, for example, can relieve severity and add grace. A curved corner or wall, a recessed ceiling with rounded edges, horizontal recessed bands of bookshelves, double or triple lines of applied metal banding on surfaces or furniture, and sofas with rounded ends all make use of the contrast of streamlining in a modern room.

Biomorphic designs in furniture, ceramics and printed textiles introduce a feeling of life in their recall of human, animal, and vegetal forms. Biomorphic designs, including amoeba-shaped cocktail tables and lamp bases, were preeminent in the 1950s. Chairs had biomorphic sides and legs, and Japanese paper lanterns in extravagant biomorphic shapes sold for a few dollars in shops specializing in Japanese imports. The influence, which by the 1960s was becoming synonymous with all that was passé, is enjoying a revival today.

Modern expands in the postwar era

Each decade of the twentieth century has added to the richness of modern design. The Great Depression and World War II put a crimp on innovation in home decorating as the world turned its attention to matters of survival in the 1930s and early 1940s.

The postwar period was a fertile era when new themes were pursued on an international scale. The birth of a new craft movement in the United States reacquainted people with the pleasures of surface decoration and ornament, softness, and humor. The

United States and its allies won the war, but the new postwar design leaders were the defeated Italy and neutral Scandinavia.

The rebirth of a vital Italian design industry was one of the surprises of the period, though perhaps it should not have been, considering Italy's reputation for outstanding design. The country experienced a burst of artistic energy, which had been stifled by the Mussolini regime. Italian craft skills and the tradition of artisans' workshops made it possible for small-scale manufacturing to start up quickly and without a great deal of capital.

The Milanese design expositions known as the Triennales resumed in 1947, becoming the leading shows in the world. Although the designers of other countries were included (the Scandinavians garnered twenty-five prizes at the Triennale of 1951), Italian firms were naturally in the spotlight.

Scandinavia emerged from the war as a design leader, too. Its clean-lined, light wood furniture and sprightly fabrics with their bright geometric abstractions suggested a rational yet cheerful environment that captured the imagination of a world weary of war and frightened by the Cold War in the 1960s and 1970s.

■ *OPPOSITE PAGE:*
Rounded sofas and curved corners or walls streamline a modern room, adding grace and relieving severity.

■ *ABOVE:*
Clean-lined, light, wooden furniture and cheerful fabrics are typical of Scandinavian design.

Courtesy of the Maytag Company

■

Arts and Crafts style can give any room a warm feeling by personalizing the space.

Neither the rationalism of the Scandinavians nor the doctrinaire rules of the International School lasted very long. By the 1960s, the enormous diversity in decoration that characterizes the present was coming into being. Some innovations of the 1960s were large, colorful geometric forms known as supergraphics and Pop Art. Geometric forms began to become more complex, and figures of people and animals and objects worked their way back into fabrics and wall coverings.

Out of a fascination with contradiction came Postmodern design, which in architecture and furniture mixes periods and influences according to the designer's personal vision or whim. A typical example of Postmodern furniture is a cabinet that looks as if it is upside down by the Italian designer Ettore Sottsass. A modern skyscraper surmounted with a pediment that looks like the top of a Chippendale chest is one of the better-known Postmodern buildings; in New York, the AT&T headquarters building was designed by Philip Johnson.

Modern today and tomorrow

Early Modernists held steadfast in their disbelief in revivals. Today, the Arts and Crafts, Art Deco, and fifties styles are considered modern. This fact alone shows there is a difference between the modern of today and the modern of yesterday. Now that almost one hundred years of twentieth-century design is behind us, the contemporary approach to the styles of the present is far more eclectic and free-spirited.

Much of the original inspiration and values remain true to the past. Still a progressive style and, if anything, even more democratic than it once was, Modernism's lasting themes include:

- Elevating function to a central place
- Controlling climate and light
- Emphasizing the relationship between indoors and outdoors with large windows
- Seating comfort
- Providing visual variety with textural contrast
- Displaying artworks made in this century
- Employing advanced materials such as plastics, machine-polished metal, and glass

Modern today has something earlier versions lacked: a recognition of a human need for ornament for both physical and psychological reasons and acceptance of the vagaries of taste as aesthetic rather than moral choices.

A designer about to create a modern item of furniture may choose to reproduce an older design, but instead of copying it exactly will change some of the detail. Perhaps a traditional wooden office chair will be executed in aluminum or a nineteenth-century wooden farm table will be done in granite. The unexpected material updates the traditional piece and is admired both for its associations with the past and its ability to portray a forward look. In a sense, modern design has come to be defined by the styles that have come before it.

Using old materials in a brand new way is also the height of modern. Recently a team of designers updated a traditional chest of drawers in natural cherry by giving the top and front an irregular and undulating edge.

■ *The use of machine-polished metal, built-in cabinetry, and streamlined ceilings satisfies the need for ornament without sacrificing simplicity.*

■ *RIGHT AND BELOW, RIGHT: The emphasis of space and the accompanying de-emphasis of clutter characterize the modern room. In addition, the use of white-and-black color schemes is typical of the contemporary effort to highlight outlines and create the illusion of greater space.*

©image/dennis krukowski; Design: Joseph Picardo Inc

©image/dennis krukowski; Courtesy Tonny Foy; Client: Laura Carpenter

Modern decorative features

FURNITURE

Straight edges and sides on pieces with little ornamentation, free-form tables in biomorphic or organic shapes, built-ins, emphasis on surface grain of wood with natural finish, light wood, chairs and tables with tubular steel or chrome legs, glass and plastic laminate tables

FLOORS

Bare wood or quarry tile with modern area rugs, wall-to-wall carpets in solid colors

WALLS

Painted white with no moldings, matte finishes, walls covered with textured unpatterned surface such as linen or burlap, glossy solid-color wall coverings, wood paneling installed on the diagonal

FABRICS

Geometric patterns, stripes, solids, nubby, soft-textured fabrics, natural materials, especially wool, linen, dull silk, and cotton

WINDOWS

Plain vertical or horizontal blinds, bare windows, simple shades, plain drapes, large expanses of glass, sliding glass doors

ACCESSORIES

Modern and primitive art, crafts, modern glass art objects, baskets or other collections grouped neatly on shelves on the wall or in an étagère

The twenty-first century

The element of surprise and familiarity demonstrated by combining the past and present in cne piece also is characteristic of interior design. As the 1990s advance, the custom of reinterpreting the past seems appropriate and is in full swing.

Every year or so, a new part of the design past is served up to the public. Often the first salvo comes in the form of a retrospective museum exhibition and a book that proffers a critical evaluation of the design theme.

The style is picked up by the fashionable decorators and their wealthy clients. The originals are bid up at auctions and fancy antiques shops. Then come magazine articles, and, in their wake, manufacturers offer reproductions that make the style available to a wider public.

Meanwhile at every step of the process there are designers and consumers figuring out how to combine the style with other design themes that are current. Finally, when all this work has revived the style, the process starts anew on something else.

■

The rooms of this open loft space are defined by groupings of furniture. In response to the increasingly limited amount of living space, homes of the twenty-first century will demand the creative treatment of multi-use areas in the home.

BIBLIOGRAPHY

DESIGN BASICS

Conran, Terence. *The House Book.* New York: Crown Publishers, 1974.
———*New House Book.* New York: Villard, 1985.
Faulkner, Sarah. *Planning a Home: A Practical Guide to Interior Design.* New York: Holt, Rinehart & Winston, 1979.
Gilliatt, Mary. *The Decorating Book.* New York: Pantheon Books, 1981.
Hampton, Mark. *Mark Hampton on Decorating.* New York: Random House, 1989.
Hope, Augustine, and Margaret Walch. *The Color Compendium.* New York: Van Nostrand Reinhold, 1990.
Pile, John. *Interior Design.* New York: Harry N. Abrams, 1988.
Rybczynski, Withold. *Home: A Short History of an Idea.* New York: Viking, 1986.

THE HEALTHY HOUSE

Bower, John. *The Healthy House.* New York: Lyle Stuart, 1989.
Hunter, Linda Mason. *The Healthy Home: An Attic-to-Basement Guide to Toxin-Free Living.* New York: Pocket Books (Simon & Schuster), 1989.
Naar, John. *Design for a Livable Planet.* New York: Harper & Row, 1990.
Pearson, David. *The Natural House Book.* New York: Simon & Schuster, 1989.

SPECIAL SUBJECTS

Cary, Jane Randolph. *How to Create Interiors for the Disabled.* New York: Pantheon Books, 1978.
Clifton-Mogg, Caroline, and Melanie Paine. *The Art and Technique of Decorating with Fabric.* New York: Prentice Hall, 1988.
Conran, Terence. *The Bed & Bath Book.* New York: Crown Publishers, 1978.
———*The Kitchen Book.* New York: Crown Publishers, 1977.
Hilliard, Elizabeth. *Finishing Touches: The Simple Details That Make all the Difference.* New York: Crown Publishers, 1990.
Irvine, Susan. *Laura Ashley Bedrooms.* New York: Harmony Books, 1988.
Lang, Donna, and Lucretia Robertson. *Decorating with Fabric.* New York: Clarkson Potter Publishers, 1986.
Lott, Jane. *Children's Rooms.* New York: Prentice Hall, 1989.
Paine, Melanie. *The Textile Art in Interior Design.* New York: Simon & Schuster, 1990.
Torrice, Antonio F., and Ro Logrippo. *In My Room: Designing for and with Children.* New York: Fawcett Columbine, 1990.
Wilhide, Elizabeth. *Laura Ashley Windows.* New York: Harmony Books, 1988.

STYLE BOOKS

Jones, Chester. *Colefax and Fowler: The Best in English Interior Deocration.* Boston: Little, Brown & Co., 1989.
Cale, Iain, and Susan Irvine. *Laura Ashley Style.* New York: Harmony Books, 1987.
Emmerling, Mary Ellisor. *American Country: A Style and Source Book.* New York: Clarkson Potter Publishers, 1980.
———*Collecting American Country.* New York, Clarkson Potter Publishers, 1983.
Freeman, Michael, Sian Evans, and Mimi Lipton. *In the Oriental Style: A Sourcebook of Decoration and Design.* Boston: Little, Brown & Co., 1990.
Madden, Chris Casson. *Interior Visions: Great American Designers and the Showcase House.* New York: Stewart, Tabori & Chang, 1988.
McCloud, Kevin. *Decorative Style.* New York: Simon & Schuster, 1990.
Moulin, Pierre, Pierre Levec, and Linda Dannenbert. *Pierre Deux's French Country.* New York: Clarkson Potter Publishers, 1984.
Sabino, Catherine. *Italian Country.* New York: Clarkson Potter Publishers, 1988.
Slesin, Suzanne, and Stafford Cliff. *English Style.* New York: Clarkson Potter Publishers, 1984.
———*French Style.* New York: Clarkson Potter Publishers, 1982.
———**and Daniel Rozensztroch.** *Japanese Style.* New York: Clarkson Potter Publishers, 1987.
———*Greek Style.* New York: Clarkson Potter Publishers, 1988.

DECORATION AND DESIGN HISTORY

Bavaro, Joseph, and Thomas L. Mossman. *The Furniture of Gustav Stickley.* New York: Prentice Hall, 1990.
Eidelberg, Martin (Editor). *Design 1935–1965: What Modern Was.* New York: Harry N. Abrams, 1991.
Gere, Charlotte. *Nineteenth-Century Decoration.* New York: Harry N. Abrams, 1989.
Gilborn, Craig. *Adirondack Furniture and the Rustic Tradition.* New York: Harry N. Abrams, 1987.
Gilliatt, Mary. *Period Style.* Boston: Little, Brown & Co., 1990.
Grier, Katherine C. *Culture and Comfort: People, Parlors, and Upholstery 1850–1930.* Rochester, N.Y.: The Strong Museum, 1988.
Guild, Robin. *The Victorian House Book.* New York: Rizzoli, 1989.
Haslam, Malcolm. *In The Nouveau Style.* Boston: Little, Brown & Co., 1989.
Leopold, Alison Kyle. *Victorian Splendor: Recreating America's 19th Century Interiors.* New York: Stewart, Tabori & Chang, 1986.
McCorquodale, Charles. *The History of the Interior.* New York: Vendome Press, 1983.
Metropolitan Museum of Art. *In Pursuit of Beauty: Americans and the Aesthetic Movement.* New York: 1987.
Moss, Roger W. *Lighting for Historic Buildings.* Washington, D.C.: National Trust for Historic Preservation.
———*Victorian Exterior Decoration: How to Paint Your 19th Century American House Historically.* New York: Henry Holt & Co., 1987.
Newman, Bruce. *Fantasy Furniture.* New York: Rizzoli, 1989.
Nylander, Jane. *Fabrics for Historic Buildings.* Washington, D.C.: National Trust for Historic Preservation.
Nylander, Richard. *Wallpapers for Historic Buildings.* Washington, D.C.: National Trust for Historic Preservation.

INDEX